THE
VEG
GROWER'S
ALMANAC

10 9 8 7 6 5 4 3 2 1

Ebury Publishing
Random House, 20 Vauxhall Bridge Road,
London, SW1V 2SA

A Penguin Random House Company

Penguin
Random House
UK

Addresses for companies within Penguin Random House can be found at:
global.penguinrandomhouse.com

This book is published to accompany the television series entitled
Gardeners' World, first broadcast on BBC2 in 2014.

Series Editor: Liz Rumbold

First published in 2014 by BBC Books, an imprint of Ebury Publishing.

www.eburypublishing.co.uk

Editorial Director: Lorna Russell
Project Editor: Louise McKeever
Copy Editor: Helena Caldon
Design and Illustrations: Two Associates
Production: Helen Everson

A CIP catalogue record for this book is available from the British Library.

ISBN 978 1 849 90782 8

Printed and bound by CPI Group (UK) Ltd, Croydon, CR0 4YY.

Penguin Random House is committed to a sustainable future for our
business, our readers and our planet. This book is made from Forest
Stewardship Council® certified paper.

Gardeners'
World

THE VEG GROWER'S ALMANAC

MARTYN COX

BBC
BOOKS

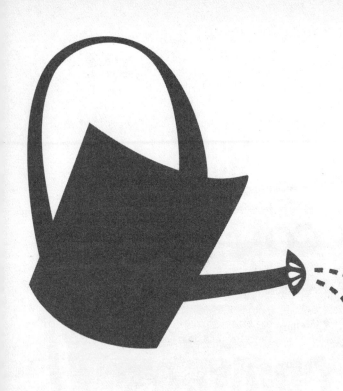

CONTENTS

INTRODUCTION

One of the greatest pleasures in life is growing your own vegetables. Peas, beans, tomatoes, salad leaves, potatoes and any other edible crops you decide to raise in your garden simply taste fresher and boast far more flavour than anything you might buy in a shop. Of course, that's not the only reason why a growing band of gardeners are starting to grow their own. Some want to cut shopping bills, reduce their carbon footprint or to simply have control over what fertilisers and pesticides (if any) are used on the crops they feed to their family. And, it's highly satisfying to see something that you've raised from seed or a young plant reach maturity and get served up on your plate as part of a delicious meal.

Whatever your motivation, there's no doubt that growing your own can sometimes be a little daunting, especially if you're fairly new to the joys of vegetable gardening - even experienced hands occasionally need help planning or advice on crops they've never grown before. As gardeners we quickly discover that there's always something that needs doing, whatever time of year it happens to be. Spring is inevitably the busiest time of year; there's a host of different crops that can be sown, young plants to be planted out and problems that have to be solved. The summer and autumn months are less frenetic, but even in the grey depths of winter, there are plants you could be growing and jobs that need doing.

And that's where this almanac will prove invaluable. Inside the pages of this little book you will find an indispensable guide to everything that you could be sowing and planting each month. All of the traditional favourites are here, such as potatoes, tomatoes, runner beans and carrots, along with herbs and less usual, up-and-coming vegetables such as tomatillos, sweet potatoes and microgreens. Everything you need to know about each crop is included, from the best varieties and sowing instructions, to looking after plants and harvesting.

But this book is much more than just a practical guide to growing your best ever vegetables. There are seasonal words of wisdom from BBC *Gardeners' World* presenter Monty Don, as well as some of his predecessors including Alan Titchmarsh, Percy Thrower and Geoff Hamilton. The book also includes sage advice passed down through the ages, quirky facts and potted histories that reveal everything you could possibly want to know about the background of some of our best known veggies. For instance, do you know what ancient civilization had a special fleet of ships to transport asparagus? Or what vegetable was treated as a substitute for ice lollies during Britain in the Second World War? If you don't, dip inside and you'll soon find out.

So, whether you've got a walled kitchen garden, allotment, vegetable patch, potager, raised bed, patio or just a window box, this book will provide you with plenty of help, advice and inspiration to make the most of whatever you've got. Oh, and hopefully it will keep you entertained along the way.

Happy gardening!

'Each year the whole garden is the scene of an unfolding drama. There is comedy, suspense and intrigue too, and occasionally tragedy. It's exciting, beguiling and ever-changing. It changes day by day, and as each season unfolds, drifting gently or arriving urgently. Within a single day the garden can go through a hundred subtle nuances.'

Carol Klein, *Life in a Cottage Garden*

If you were to ask any vegetable gardener to nominate their favourite month of the year, it's unlikely many would say January. Who could blame them? The weather can often be grim at the turn of the year, providing very little reason for most of us to step foot outside. Fortunately, there's no need to worry about how things are getting on out there in your absence, or fret that you'll have to play catch up when the weather improves. Why? Well, simply because there isn't very much that needs doing.

So take advantage of nature's pause in proceedings. Few of us get a chance to scrutinise seed catalogues during December because we're so busy making preparations for Christmas, so use the opportunity in this quiet month to go through them thoroughly. Make a long list of what you want to grow, then edit it down to something more manageable, before finally placing your order. Don't just go for the same old varieties each year, keep things interesting by trying a few different varieties or crops alongside some of your favourites.

If you are feeling guilty after a spate of overindulgence during the festive period, and if conditions are suitable, by all means finish off winter-digging bare patches of soil, or spread well-rotted compost or garden compost over beds. An hour's physical work will soon help you to burn a few calories and keep you warm on a bitterly cold day. However, this won't always be possible – be guided by the weather; it's impossible to turn solid, frozen soil, and walking on soggy earth will only compact it, damaging its structure and making more work for you in spring.

This month is all about preparation and planning so you can begin forcing chicory, get your potatoes ready for planting after the frosts and get a grip on weeds before spring sets them off through your plot. January is the time to ease yourself into a new year of gardening with a few gentle jobs.

ORDERING SEEDS

Last month, the seed catalogues fell thick and fast through the letterbox as nurseries unveiled their lists of tried-and-tested varieties, along with a host of brand-new ones that they hope we'll try.

It's a time-honoured tradition among gardeners to cheer themselves up on the bleakest of winter days by planning what to grow in a few months' time. Nothing beats sitting down inside with a mug of something hot and with catalogues spread out in front of you, or with your PC, laptop or tablet propped up in front of you with online catalogues in full glorious colour.

Armed with a pen and paper, make separate lists of the different salads, root crops, beans, brassicas, herbs and other vegetables you want to grow. Begin with lots, then edit down the list to something more reasonable. Like a child in a sweet shop, it's all too easy to get carried away and order far too much, only to discover later on that you don't have the time or space to sow everything. It can be a costly mistake.

There are no hard and fast rules about what you should order. However, it's best to grow crops that you or your family like to eat, or that are expensive to buy in the shops or impossible to find unless you go to a specialist food store. Select plants that are suitable for the style or size of your growing space – if you have a tiny courtyard or patio, go for compact vegetables or varieties suitable for raising in pots, but if you have a larger area for growing vegetables, you can be more ambitious.

If you're new to growing vegetables, there's nothing wrong with ordering a selection of traditional varieties that have been grown by generations of gardeners. Depending on the weather, and you, they are more or less guaranteed to give good results. Seasoned vegetable growers should keep things exciting by including a few varieties or edibles they've never tried before, or by adding a handful of newcomers to their list.

CROP ROTATION

When planning what to grow, bear in mind the traditional technique of crop rotation. This involves growing separate types of annual vegetables in a different bed or patch of soil each year. This technique is used for a number of reasons: it prevents your soil from being sapped of nutrients by the same plants year after year; it reduces the chance of pests and diseases building up in the same spot, and allows plants to take up any nutrients helpfully left behind in the soil by others. Put some time aside to make a plan on paper and keep it in a safe place so you can refer to it when the time comes to start sowing.

There are numerous different ways of rotating your crops, but the easiest is to work on a three-year cycle. Apart from perennials, which will remain in the same position, divide everything else into three main groups:

- **Beans, peas (legumes) and fruiting vegetables** – runner beans, broad beans, French beans, peas, tomatoes, peppers, aubergines, courgettes and sweetcorn, etc.
- **Brassicas** – cabbages, broccoli, kale, swedes, Brussels sprouts and cauliflowers, etc.
- **Root vegetables and salads** – potatoes, spinach, beetroots, carrots, sweet potatoes, onions, lettuce and spring onions, etc.

In year one, give each group a designated bed or area. In year two, grow brassicas in the space left by the beans (beans absorb nitrogen from the air and trap the nutrient in their roots. After the crop dies, nitrogen resides in the soil and can be taken up by the hungry brassicas). Grow root vegetables in the gap left by brassicas, and beans in the position formerly taken by root vegetables. Rotate again in year three. In year four, the vegetables should be back in their original positions.

FORCING CHICORY

The tightly packed, tender, blanched heads of chicory, known as chicons, are a cold-weather treat – the crisp, slightly bitter leaves are delicious in winter salads, tossed into a stir-fry or sautéed with butter. They are widely available in the shops, but are also easy to produce at home.

Grow 'Witloof de Brussels' or another variety that is suitable for forcing, sowing seeds in July or August for winter forcing. Lift the roots of several plants and pot up in a large container filled with compost (obviously, you can skip this step if you are already growing chicory in pots). Cut back tops to leave 2.5cm of stubby growth above the crown. Cover the pot with a bucket or another pot, making sure you cover up drainage holes with black polythene to block out all light – it's important to eliminate every chink or the leaves could turn green and taste overly bitter. Place in a cool, dark, frost-free place under cover. The chicons should be ready for harvesting when they are about 15cm tall, usually within a month.

DID YOU KNOW?

The technique of forcing chicory was discovered by chance in 1830. A Belgian farmer noticed white chicons growing on the roots of chicory stored in his cellar. During the 1850s, horticulturists at the Botanical Garden of Brussels refined a method for forcing chicory and the first commercial crop was sold at the capital's vegetable market in 1867. Today, it's the second most popular vegetable in Belgium – an average of 7kg is eaten per person, each year.

GROWING POTATOES

Most people could name a handful of different potato varieties, but few, if any, would be able to list the 250 or so different ones that are available to UK gardeners. These come in many different shapes, colours and sizes – from those that were around when our great, great-grandfathers were gardening, to modern varieties that have been bred for higher yields and their resistance to diseases. All of them are a doddle to grow and are started from seed potatoes – special tubers that are certified to be free of diseases. Potatoes are perfect for planting in the ground or in pots, making them ideal for even the smallest of spaces.

Different types

So a potato is just a potato? Not really. They are divided into different groups based on when they are ready to harvest. First early potatoes can be dug up from early to midsummer, when they are about the size of hens' eggs. Second early potatoes are usually ready when their flowers start to open, from midsummer onwards. Maincrop potatoes can be lifted from September into October – eat them straightaway or store them in paper sacks for winter use.

Some potatoes to try

- **First early** – 'Swift', 'Rocket', 'Pentland Javelin'
- **Second early** – 'Kestrel', 'Yukon Gold', 'Maris Peer'
- **Maincrop** – 'King Edward', 'Desiree', 'Valor'

'Chitting' potatoes

Prior to planting, coax seed potatoes into producing shoots using a simple technique known as chitting. Stand tubers on a shallow tray lined with newspaper or place a single one in each cup of an empty cardboard egg carton. Make sure the rose end is facing upwards (this is the part marked with a cluster of indentations or 'eyes', where the sprouts will grow). Place in a greenhouse, porch, unheated spare room or another cool, light, dry place for about six weeks until they have produced lots of 2.5cm-long, stubby green shoots. Avoid putting them in a warm, dark place, such as a cupboard, or in a very light spot such as a south-facing windowsill, or you will end up with lots of spindly white shoots that will snap off easily.

Planting in the ground

Potatoes thrive in fertile, well-drained soil that gets plenty of sunshine. Place a single tuber in a 15cm-deep hole, making sure the shoots are facing upwards. Space earlies 30cm apart, with 60cm between rows; second earlies and maincrop varieties 45cm apart, with 70cm between rows. Gently cover with soil and water them in. Potatoes get thirsty, so give them plenty of water, especially during dry weather. When the stems are 20cm high, use a rake to draw soil around the foliage to leave just the tops showing. Known as 'earthing up', this blocks out light into the roots and prevents the growing potatoes turning green and inedible.

Growing in pots

Potatoes are easy to grow in large pots, fabric vegetable planters or even used compost bags. Space three to five tubers on a 10cm layer of multi-purpose compost and cover with another 10cm layer of compost. Water well. When stems are 20cm tall, cover them to half their height with compost. Continue to add more compost as the stems grow taller, stopping when you are 10cm away from the top of the container.

Potato problems

Blight can be a big problem in warm, wet summers. The disease leads to brown patches appearing on the plants' leaves, which is followed by white fungal growth. The stems will eventually collapse. Underground, brown sunken patches develop on tubers. For best prevention, ensure you earth up tubers deeply and, if you are a non-organic gardener, spray the plants with a recommended copper-based fungicide as a precaution if weather conditions favour the disease. Remove infected plants, including tubers, to restrict its spread. Some varieties are bred to have a degree of blight resistance, and some varieties are particularly prone to the disease, so choose your tubers carefully.

Slugs are a common pest of potatoes. Damage to the foliage is superficial, rather than detrimental to the crop, but soil-dwelling keeled slugs will eat holes in tubers. A thin scattering of organic slug pellets around plants on heavy, wet soil will help. Damage can be limited by lifting tubers as soon as they are ready, rather than leaving them in the ground.

Common scab is a problem when conditions are very dry or the soil is particularly alkaline. The organism causes rough, raised patches to develop on the skin of potatoes. It's largely cosmetic and the unsightly 'scabs' are removed when peeling. To avoid problems, dig in plenty of garden compost prior to planting to improve the soil's ability to hold on to moisture. Keep plants well watered during dry spells.

A little bit of history

Bangers and mash, shepherd's pie, chips and a host of other British classics rely on potatoes as a core ingredient, but this root vegetable is not a native of our shores. Known botanically as *Solanum tuberosum*, potatoes were first cultivated in South America back in 5000BC and were introduced into Europe by the Spanish in the 1560s. Generations of primary school children have grown up thinking that Sir Walter Raleigh brought them to Britain in the 1580s, but some experts reckon Sir John Hawkins, an admiral in Queen Elizabeth I's navy, beat him to it by almost 20 years. Initially, potatoes were treated with contempt or curiosity, and even peasants refused to eat the tubers. It wasn't until the mid-eighteenth century that they became a staple part of our diet. By the late 1800s there were many named varieties, some of which are still in cultivation today.

Heritage spuds

If you hear a foodie talking about heritage or heirloom potatoes, they're referring to varieties that were introduced prior to 1951. People seek out these old-timers for a number of reasons; some consider them to have a superior flavour to modern potatoes, while others like growing them because of their interesting

TOP TIP

When storing potatoes, place a few apples close by – the ethylene gas emitted by the fruit prevents tubers sprouting.

history. Their appearance is often unique; perhaps having an unusual shape or a skin that's a striking colour. Garden centres may offer a couple of varieties, vegetable specialists even more, but for the greatest choice of antique tubers it's worth visiting a potato day event, which are held around the country in January and February. Get there early. Some varieties are very rare and only a few tubers will be available for sale.

10 HISTORIC POTATOES TO TRY

1 **Pink Fir Apple 1850**
   Really unusual, long, knobbly, pink-skinned tubers.

2 **Belle de Fontenay 1885**
   A classic, yellow-skinned French salad potato.

3 **British Queen 1894**
   White potato named in honour of Queen Victoria.

4 **Epicure 1897**
   White-skinned, bred in Hampshire for Suttons Seeds.

5 **Sharpe's Express 1900**
   Percy Thrower's favourite potato.

6 **Edzell Blue 1915**
   Striking blue skin and white flesh.

7 **Arran Victory 1918**
   Purple skin contrasting with white flesh.

8 **Catriona 1920**
   Yellow skin with purple splashes.

9 **Arran Consul 1925**
   Popular during Second World War.

10 **Red Duke of York 1942**
   Red skin, attractive foliage and flowers.

WEED CONTROL

Annual weeds are a problem in gardens, allotments and just about anywhere else you grow vegetables – they can even colonise the tops of pots. Apart from looking unsightly, they can hinder the growth or final yield of your edible crops by competing for water, nutrients, space and light. Some harbour pests and diseases, which can spread to healthy ornamental or edible plants. Many weeds flower and set seed all year round, so it's a good idea to spend a few minutes each week keeping on top of them. In January, when there's not that much to do in the garden, really give the ground a blitz so there's less weeding to do in spring. You can keep on top of most annuals by hand-pulling or hoeing, without needing to resort to other forms of control.

The fearful five

1 **Hairy bittercress** (*Cardamine hirsuta*) is a rosette-forming annual weed with white flowers on 15cm stalks. It will quickly colonise an empty space thanks to its seed pods, which explode to spread the contents far and wide. A single seed pod can carry 30 seeds and an average plant can contain over 600! It's easy to pull up the plants by hand or by hoeing as the weed is so shallow rooted – don't leave them on the surface of the soil after removing, though, as the pods can still ripen and release their seeds.

2 **Sun spurge** (*Euphorbia helioscopia*) is an ankle-high annual weed topped with lime-green flowers from late spring to mid-October. It spreads itself around the garden via its near-indestructible seeds, which have been found to remain viable underground for over 20 years. Closely related to ornamental euphorbias, it exudes a white milky sap (known as latex) that can irritate those with sensitive skin. Remove with a hoe or wear gloves if you want to pull them up by hand.

3 Fat hen (*Chenopodium album*) can grow to 1m tall or more, with stems clothed with triangular-shaped leaves covered with a powdery white coating – these often, but not always, have attractively toothed margins. This annual weed flowers between July and September, with an average plant capable of releasing 20,000 seeds. Try to keep it under control by removing plants before they get the chance to set seed.

4 Groundsel (*Senecio vulgaris*) is a pretty little annual weed with scallop-edged leaves and lots of small, bright yellow flowers. Its main flowering period is from mid-spring to mid-October, but it can produce flowers and set seed all year round – a large plant can jettison 38,000 seeds. Apart from being able to quickly colonise empty space it can also act as a host to aphids, virus and rust disease, which can overwinter on its foliage before spreading to garden plants. Remove young plants by hand before they seed.

5 Annual meadow grass (*Poa annua*) can form a dense carpet over time and is often a problem on allotments, although it can occur just about anywhere. Most grasses spread via runners, but this one flowers and disperses its seeds just about all year round. It can be difficult to tug up by hand, especially if there is a large patch to remove, but hoeing regularly will help to keep it under control.

DID YOU KNOW?

Hairy bitter cress is a member of the mustard family and its edible leaves are sometimes added to salads or blitzed into pesto by foragers. The leaves of fat hen are high in vitamin C, and this plant was widely eaten in this country from Neolithic times until the sixteenth century.

'Where people usually go wrong is that they take on far more than they can manage then can't keep up with the work. The result is that their crops are ruined and their time has been wasted. If you were to ask me for my top kitchen-gardening tip, I'd say that you'd do far better to grow half the amount, but grow it twice as well.'

Alan Titchmarsh, *The Kitchen Gardener*

There is a sense of change in the air this month. Although snow storms, sleet, incessant rain, icy winds and hard frosts are all too common at this time of year, winter's grip is definitely beginning to loosen. In February, the days become noticeably longer and a period of inclement weather that restricts our activities outside can just as easily be followed by a few days of glorious sunshine – offering a hint of what is, fingers crossed, just around the corner.

....

In the garden, a few brave, early flowering bulbs and shrubs with blooms that infuse the air with a delightful perfume on a still day invigorate our spirits when we are tempted to pull on our boots and step through the back door. Use the time to finish off winter-digging when weather conditions permit, improving the soil by adding plenty of garden compost or well-rotted manure. If you want to get ahead, there are seeds and sets you can sow and plant this month, too, but only if the conditions are right. If they're not, don't despair – there's no harm in waiting, or if you have the room, start them off in small pots under cover for planting out later.

If you placed an order for seeds last month (or even earlier if you were really organised!), make the most of any spare time by sorting through them so you are prepared for sowing. Try and arrange them into groups, such as herbs, salads, root crops and so on, then put each of these categories in sowing sequence. Store them in an old shoebox, wooden seed tray or something similar, to keep them tidy. It might also pay to make a list of what you're going to sow and when.

JERUSALEM ARTICHOKES

This vegetable is rarely found in supermarkets, but the knobbly tubers of Jerusalem artichoke are so tasty that it's worth growing them – they pack a warm, nutty flavour that can be enjoyed by roasting, blitzing into a purée or cooked into a soup.

Plant tubers between late February and April in a sunny or partly shaded part of the garden in well-drained soil – dig individual holes 10cm deep, 30cm apart. When stems are around 30cm tall, draw soil around them to a depth of 15cm to help stabilise the plants as they grow. You may need to provide extra support with stakes to prevent the tops being blown about if your garden is exposed or windy.

Although they're mainly grown for their edible tubers, Jerusalem artichokes boast ornamental good looks above ground too. They produce towering stems topped with attractive yellow flowers that make a good alternative to helenium or rudbeckia at the back of a border, or they can be used to make a screen that is both flowering and edible.

Prune back the stems in autumn to 8cm high when the foliage starts to turn yellow. You can harvest the tubers with a garden fork as required between late autumn and winter.

Be aware that Jerusalem artichokes can be invasive. If you don't want them coming back the following year, make sure you remove every last tuber to prevent them spreading.

What to grow

- **Fuseau** – is a traditional French variety with long, smooth, white tubers that are easier to peel than most.
- **Originals** – produces roundish tubers that resemble large pebbles with a deep, smoky flavour. Its flower stems can reach 3m in height.
- **Gerard** – was bred in France and is popular with restaurants for its smoky flavour. The roundish red tubers surround pure white flesh.

A little bit of history

Its name may suggest it comes from the Middle East, but this knobbly tuber actually originated in North America. There are many theories about how the Jerusalem artichoke got its common name, but nobody really knows for certain. Known botanically as *Helianthus tuberosus*, this vegetable is a member of the aster family and can produce towering stems topped with small, sunflower-like blooms in summer. Native Americans were the first to cultivate the plants, which were introduced to Europe by French explorer Samuel de Champlain in 1616. The Jerusalem artichoke arrived in Britain the following year.

Although the nutty flavoured tubers are considered to be a delicacy, the vegetable does suffer from a reputation for causing flatulence, which has led to some dubbing the vegetable 'fartichokes'. Even in 1621, just four years after it was introduced here, an edition of John Gerard's *The Herball* suggested these vegetables were better fed to pigs than humans, because 'they stirre and cause a filthie loathsome stinking wind within the bodie, thereby causing the body to be pained and tormented'.

SPROUTING SEEDS INDOORS

If the weather's too bitter to go outdoors, raise a crop of sprouting seeds from the comfort of your home. All you need is a space on a well-lit, but not sunny, windowsill, and you'll soon be harvesting handfuls of tasty sprouts to add to salads, stir-fries, sandwiches and other dishes.

Looking exactly as their name suggests, these are seeds that are eaten when they have produced a small sprout. Seed companies offer a large range of plants that are suitable for sprouting, from individual varieties to mixes. This includes mung bean and soy seeds, whose sprouts are those most often found in supermarkets, to less commonly eaten varieties such as sunflower sprouts.

There are various ways of growing sprouts; some people like to use bags or jam jars covered with muslin, and there are also many different gadgets available for the purpose in health-food shops. For ease of use, though, you can't beat a traditional two-tier device, which consists of a tray at the bottom to catch excess water and two clear trays that sit on top of each other.

Growing the seeds couldn't be easier. Soak them in water overnight, then spread them across the bottom of one of your clear trays. To prevent them going mouldy or tasting horrible, 'wash' seeds daily with some fresh water, allowing it to drain away.

Depending on what you're growing, expect to be eating your own tasty sprouts anywhere between two to eight days after sowing.

10 tasty sprouts

1 Adzuki beans **2** Alfalfa **3** Broccoli **4** Chickpea **5** Fenugreek
6 Mustard **7** Red cabbage **8** Rocket **9** Spring onions
10 Sunflowers

GROW SHALLOTS

Shallots are the gourmet cousin of onions, with superior-flavoured bulbs that can be chopped into salads, pickled or added to many savoury dishes. Apart from being good to eat, shallots are easy to grow from sets – small, immature bulbs that can be planted in the autumn (November) to overwinter in the ground, or planted from mid-February until the middle of March. Make sure the sets you buy have been heat-treated, which will prevent them bolting and going to seed too early.

Planting in the ground

Prepare the soil by digging it over and raking to leave a crumbly finish. Cover the soil with a low plastic tunnel or cloche to warm it for a couple of weeks, then remove it and make holes with a dibber – 15cm apart in each row, with 23cm between rows. Plant the shallots so that their noses are just peeking above the surface. Firm the soil around them with your fingertips and water well.

Planting in pots

Choose a big pot or another container that can accommodate plenty of bulbs – an old wooden storage crate that's at least 24cm deep and 60cm wide would be ideal. Fill with soil-based compost, such as John Innes No. 3, and plant as you would in the ground.

Looking after plants

Water shallots if the weather is dry and give them an occasional feed with a general liquid fertiliser. Spread a mulch around the plants to conserve moisture and keep down weeds, or plant them through weed-suppressant matting. A light feed of sulphate of potash in June will help ripen the bulbs ready for harvesting at the end of summer, when the leaves sag and turn brown.

Harvesting

Lift bulbs carefully from the ground with a fork, taking care not to damage them. Remove as much soil as possible and allow the bulbs to dry off in the sun until the outer skin is papery. If the weather is wet, place them on a wire rack in a light spot indoors.

Storing

Shallots will keep for around eight months if placed in a cool, dry place. Either spread them out in a tray or store them in a net bag – this can be hung up in a shed or garage.

Problems

Shallots are prone to the same problems as onions – rot and mildew – but recently planted sets are also very tempting for foraging birds, who may pull them out of the ground. Check them regularly and refirm them into the ground if necessary.

Fantastic shallots to try

- **Golden Gourmet** – produces a heavy yield of large, brown-skinned bulbs and is slow to bolt.
- **Mikor** – is an elliptical-shaped French variety with reddish skin and white-pink flesh. It's great for storing.
- **Pesandor** – has a long, slender shape that makes it perfect for slicing into salads.
- **Pikant Red** – was bred in Holland and has medium-sized red bulbs with a strong, spicy flavour.
- **Red Sun** – forms a spherical bulb with red skin surrounding white flesh. It's great chopped into salads or for pickling.

FOODIE FACT

First served in 1836, the classic French béarnaise sauce is made by reducing shallots in white wine vinegar, before adding tarragon and chervil, then thickening with egg yolk and butter.

SLUG AND SNAIL CONTROL

There are many garden pests, but none are as pernicious as slugs and snails. Year after year they top the Royal Horticultural Society's Top 10 pest chart because they are found in nearly all gardens and are not particularly fussy about what they eat.

In the vegetable patch they'll munch on stems, chomp their way through succulent leaves and take chunks out of cucumbers, courgettes and the outer shells of beans. Some live in the soil and will burrow into potatoes, leaving them riddled with holes. Young plants are extremely vulnerable to their appetite and it's not unknown for recently planted seedlings to be razed to the ground overnight.

Slugs are active all year round, while some snails will hunker down in a sheltered place over winter and generally wake up late in the season. At this time, snails are starting to think about mating and many gardeners heed the old wives' tale of making sure control measures are in place by 14 February, Valentine's Day, to prevent an unwanted population boom.

Keeping them under control

There are countless ways of controlling slugs and snails, with some methods having greater success than others. Barriers can be effective, such as spreading coffee grounds, crushed egg shells or sharp grit around the base of plants. Copper rings or tapes also have their plaudits – the metal repels the pests with a tiny jolt of static electricity.

Slug pellets containing metaldehyde have long been used by gardeners, but there is concern over the impact they have on beneficial wildlife. If you are gardening organically, use those made from iron phosphate which have been approved for the purpose and will break down over time, adding nutrients to the soil.

Products containing microscopic nematodes have become more popular in recent years. A powder containing the predator is mixed with water and then sprinkled onto the soil to seek out slugs. The only drawback with this method is that the nematodes will only kill slugs that are under or in contact with the soil, and not any surface-dwelling snails.

Hunting them down

Among the best techniques to keep your plants free of slugs is to inspect your garden regularly and despatch any that you find. Check upturned pots, gaps in walls, under tables and the backs of leaves. Some patrol their plot at night, going out with a torch so they can collect the pests when they are at their most active.

DID YOU KNOW?

There are around 30 different types of slug in the UK and an average garden is thought to contain around 200 of the slithery pests per cubic metre. By far the most damaging is the common grey field slug, which mainly feeds on plants above ground and has the potential to produce up to 90,000 grandchildren in its lifetime – which can be up to five years!

Snail Sat Nav

An amateur scientist from Devon discovered that snails have a homing instinct and can return to the same spot even if moved up to 10 metres away.

↑ GET A HEAD START ON VEGETABLES

If you've got a heated greenhouse, it's a shame not to make the most of all the bench space inside. Most people will start sowing their veg seeds in spring, but if you have the advantage of a protected structure, you can get a head start by sowing some tender crops in late winter.

There are many benefits to sowing early: by starting plants off indoors you will often gain four to six weeks of growing time over seeds sown directly into the ground, and as a result you should enjoy earlier, heavier crops than those that are sown later. Starting early is also beneficial to sun-loving Mediterranean crops that need a long growing season to produce a decent yield.

Tomatoes, aubergines, cucumbers, basil and all kinds of peppers can be started off this month by sowing seeds in pots and trays that are placed in a heated propagator – this is an essential device for raising plants at this time of year. Some are narrow enough to fit on a windowsill, while others have a much larger capacity and may be equipped with a fixed thermostat or one that's adjustable to control the heat. A temperature between 18–21°C is ideal for germinating most seeds.

If you don't have a greenhouse, be wary about starting seeds too early. Most seedlings will soon need individual pots and these will quickly fill up a windowsill or sunny positions indoors. Remember, the seeds will need to remain under cover until there's no longer any danger from frost, which can mean two or three months, depending on when you sow and your local climate. During this time as they grow they may need to be moved into larger pots, putting more pressure on your space. If you run out of room or conditions become too cramped, their growth could be arrested. Of course, this shouldn't put you off, just pick a few key varieties and be judicious over the amount of seeds you sow in relation to the space you have available.

SPROUTING BROCCOLI

The tender flower heads of this vegetable don't only taste good, they're also packed full of vitamins and nutrients. Seeds can be sown straight into the ground outdoors in spring, but are arguably best started indoors to ensure successful germination – any time between February and April is ideal.

Sowing seeds

Sow several seeds in small pots or a seed tray and cover with a 2cm layer of finely sifted compost – don't get too carried away, six plants will provide enough tasty flowering shoots to feed a family of four, so only sow a few more seeds than needed to cover any losses. When seedlings are large enough to handle, carefully prick them out into individual 9cm pots. Grow them on under cover until safe to plant out – when there's no longer any danger of frost.

Planting and growing

Space young plants 60cm apart, with a gap of 60cm between rows. Water regularly until established. Once the plants get going, don't overwater but keep the soil damp. As the broccoli grows it will become top heavy – earth up the stems to provide support. It may be necessary to shore them up with small stakes in autumn if they're in a windy position.

Harvesting

Sprouting broccoli shoots should be ready for harvesting from winter into spring. Harvest a few on a regular basis to encourage more shoots to form – it should be possible to keep picking from the same plant for around two months. Snap them off when they're about 15cm long and the buds are still closed.

Try these varieties

'Early White Sprouting' has sweet, white flower shoots, while 'Early Purple Sprouting' has attractive purple heads. 'Italian Green Sprouting' forms lots of green heads.

IS IT BROCCOLI?

Mention broccoli and many people think of the vegetable with large, round heads similar to a cauliflower. In fact, this is calabrese; sprouting broccoli is the type that produces lots of smaller florets.

CULTURE VULTURE

Former US president George Bush Snr. wasn't a big fan of broccoli. In 1990 he banned it from being served on Air Force One, the presidential plane. 'I do not like broccoli. And I haven't liked it since I was a little kid and my mother made me eat it. And I'm President of the United States and I'm not going to eat any more broccoli,' he said.

RAISED BEDS

A raised bed is essentially a giant container that allows you to grow a wide range of vegetables in a fairly confined and manageable space. Generally consisting of a square or rectangular frame filled with a compost mix, they can be easily put together from old bricks, untreated railway sleepers or lengths of timber. Another option is to buy an off-the-shelf kit that can be screwed or slotted together.

A single raised bed makes an attractive feature in a small garden and is a good use of space, allowing you to easily take care of a lot of crops in a designated area – raising the same number of vegetables in pots would take up a lot a room and require more careful management, especially when it comes to watering.

Raised beds are ideal on allotments or larger vegetable patches. They make it easy to plan crop-rotation programmes and allow you to grow vegetables on boggy ground or on clay soils – which tend to remain soggy in winter and dry rock-solid in summer – by being able to improve the soil within the bed. As a bonus, raised beds demand less maintenance than open plots – paths in between the beds can be covered with strips of landscape fabric and then spread with bark chippings or gravel, reducing the area that needs weeding.

Beds measuring 2.4m by 1.2m are ideal, as you need to be able to easily reach into the centre for harvesting without having to walk across them, compacting the soil in the process. Aim for a minimum depth of 15cm, but if you want to grow root crops, such as carrots and parsnips, the sides of the bed will need to be around 30cm, while potatoes need beds about 40cm deep. There are no set rules about what you must use to fill the bed, but a mixture of topsoil and garden compost works well.

AUBERGINES

To perform well in this country, aubergines need a long growing season and plenty of warmth. Sow plants early and raise them under cover for more robust specimens.

Sowing seeds

Scatter a few seeds in 7.5cm pots and cover with a fine layer of vermiculite. Water and place in a heated propagator. Once germinated, remove the pots and keep the seedlings damp. When large enough, prick out each seedling into its own pot.

Growing on

Keep the young plants in a warm, frost-free place, such as a windowsill or heated greenhouse. When roots begin to show through the pots drainage holes, move into 12cm pots filled with multi-purpose compost. When plants are about 20cm tall, or before if they start to lean, stake them with a small cane. Finish by potting into a 30cm container. When they are 30cm high, pinch out the tip of the main stem to produce bushier plants.

Inside or outside?

Plants can go outside from the end of May or beginning of June, but they will need gradual acclimatising to life outdoors before they stay outside permanently. If you have the space, keep them in a greenhouse and they should perform better than those positioned outdoors due to the extra warmth.

What to grow

There is great variety among aubergines. 'Moneymaker' has classic glossy black fruits and 'Violetta Lunga' is an Italian variety with long purple fruit. For something a bit different try cylindrical white 'Snowy', red-skinned 'Red Egg' or 'Rosa Bianca', whose fruit are red and pink with white shading.

'There comes a time every
year, somewhere between
the middle of March and the
first week of April, when
I am possessed by my garden.
It runs through my veins like
a dancing river, occupies my
sleep with dreams that sprout
new leaves, and distracts
me from honest labour.
I am bewitched by spring.'

Monty Don, *Gardening at Longmeadow*

By now, you could be forgiven for thinking that winter is going to just keep reminding us that it's not over yet, but the welcome arrival of March signals the rise of spring – a time when gardens, and some gardeners, seem to wake up from hibernation. Early flowering bulbs light up patches of empty soil, swollen buds adorn once-naked branches and the grass starts to actively grow. It's an unstoppable metamorphosis that lifts our spirits and motivates even the most fair-weather gardener into action.

Sadly, the weather doesn't always acknowledge that the seasons have changed; hard frosts, snow showers and bitterly cold winds are just as likely this month as those mild, sunny days when you can step outdoors without a coat or hat to keep you snug. Yet on the whole, temperatures are on the rise and are often quite pleasant by the end of the month, when the clocks go forward an hour, rewarding us with lighter mornings and evenings.

It's inevitable that after months of near inactivity in the vegetable garden, especially if we're enjoying a mild spell, you'll be itching to start sowing. The good news is that tender vegetables, such as tomatoes, peppers and aubergines, can be started off indoors. Those gardening in mild regions or with free-draining soil that warms up early can sow broad beans, cabbages, peas and other hardier plants outdoors. Resist the temptation if you live in a colder part of the country; you're better off waiting until the end of the month or early into the next before making a start.

PLANTING ASPARAGUS

Asparagus is a gourmet vegetable that commands high prices in shops during its growing season, which is from late April to the end of June. If you have the space, this perennial vegetable is surprisingly straightforward to grow and will reward you with succulent spears for up to 20 years.

The perfect site

Asparagus thrives in full sun and well-drained soil, but needs some protection from the wind. There's no point growing it in a small garden; for a worthwhile crop, you should plant it in a dedicated bed, allotment or raised bed. Clear the bed of weeds and scatter some general fertiliser granules over the area a week or so before planting. Fork it in and rake the site level.

Planting

Start with one-year-old dormant plants, known as crowns. Dig a trench, 30cm wide by 20cm deep, and work in some well-rotted manure to the bottom. Cover the base with a 5cm layer of soil. Make a 10cm-high ridge of soil down the centre of the trench and place the crowns on top. Space them 30cm apart, spreading the roots out evenly either side of the ridge. Replace the soil until the bud tips are just visible. Leave 45cm between rows, staggering the plants against the adjacent rows. Water the bed and mulch with garden compost or well-rotted manure.

Harvesting

Stop yourself picking any spears that appear in the first year or you'll weaken the crowns. Most varieties can be picked two years after planting. To harvest spears, wait until they are about 12cm long and remove them with a serrated knife, cutting 2.5cm beneath the soil. Stop cutting in mid-June to allow plants to build up their energy for next year.

Looking after plants

Keep the bed free of weeds and spread some general fertiliser granules over the ground in spring. After harvesting, the remaining stems will grow taller; allow the ferny fronds to remain until they turn yellow later in the year, then cut down all the spears to ground level.

Good varieties to try

- **Gijnlim F1** – harvest spears a year after planting.
- **Connover's Collosal** – dark green spears with a purple head.
- **Jersey Knight** – thick, tender spears.
- **Pacific Purple** – purple spears.
- **Backlim** – thick, green spears.

DID YOU KNOW?

White asparagus, grown in tunnels without sunlight, is a more popular vegetable in France, Germany and the Netherlands than green asparagus.

CULTURE VULTURE

Asparagus is the real name of Gus, the theatre cat,
in T.S Eliot's *Old Possum's Book of Practical Cats*.

A little bit of history

Asparagus is native to parts of the Eastern Mediterranean and
has been cultivated for over 2000 years. The ancient Romans
prized this vegetable and a special fleet of ships was created to
transport it from the north of Italy down to Rome. It was first
grown in Britain during the sixteenth century and has long
been considered an aphrodisiac. Way back in 1633, herbalist
John Gerard wrote in his *The Herball* that eating asparagus was
'thought to increase seed, and stir up lust' and in nineteenth-
century France, bridegrooms were even served a three-course
meal containing asparagus at their wedding supper to get them
in the mood. Apart from its supposed power for getting pulses
racing, asparagus is also a potent source of fibre, potassium and
folic acid, and contains vitamins A, B and C.

GROWING PEPPERS

Sweet peppers have become much more popular in
recent years, but their more fiery relative, chilli peppers,
have attained cult status and are even celebrated at festivals
held around the country. Both are easy to grow. Seeds will
germinate easily indoors, resulting in young plants that will
be ready to go outside in late spring – they can be planted in
the vegetable patch, but are ideally suited to pots. Place them
in a sunny, sheltered spot and they'll romp away, producing
masses of attractive fruits that will be ready for harvesting from
midsummer until the end of September.

Sowing seeds

Fill a small pot with good-quality seed compost, flatten it down
to leave a level surface, then sow a few seeds on top. Cover with a
fine layer of vermiculite, water and place in a heated propagator.
After the seeds have germinated, remove the pot from the
propagator and place on a light windowsill or on the bench in a
heated greenhouse. When they are 2cm tall, move each seedling
into its own 10cm pot.

Early days

When roots begin to show through the bottom of the pots,
transfer them to 12cm pots filled with multi-purpose compost.
When plants are about 20cm tall, or before if they start to lean,
stake them with a pea stick. Pinch out the tops of peppers when
they are about 30cm tall to encourage lots of side branches.
Plants are ready to go outside in late May or when all danger of
frost has passed.

Looking after them

For a bumper crop make sure you water regularly, especially
in hot weather, and feed every two weeks with a high-potash
fertiliser. Feeding should start when the flowers first appear,
usually while plants are still indoors, and needs to continue until
all the fruit has been harvested.

Harvesting

The fruits are generally ready for harvesting from July and can
be removed from plants with a sharp knife or secateurs. Pick
them regularly to encourage plants to put their energy into
producing more fruit.

Most seeds will germinate,
so only sow one or two more
than you need in case of losses.

Some great chilli peppers to grow

- **Jalapeno** – the classic pizza pepper.
- **Norfolk Naga** – caution! Extra hot fruit!
- **Hungarian Hot Wax** – medium-hot, conical peppers.
- **Cayenne** – long, slender, red pods.
- **Tricolor Variegata** – variegated leaves, purple fruit that turn red.

And some sweet peppers too...

- **Corno di Toro Rosso** – long, tapering pepper from Italy.
- **California Wonder** – thick-skinned green and red peppers.
- **Bell Boy F1** – blocky, red and green fruit.
- **Mohawk F1** – green fruit that ripens to bright yellow.
- **Gourmet** – sweet, bright orange fruit.

What's the Scoville scale?

The heat sensation of chillies is caused by a compound called capsaicin, the amount of which within different varieties is measured on the Scoville Heat Scale. This measure was invented in 1912 by Wilbur Scoville, an American pharmacist. At the lower end of the scale, peppers can taste mildly spicy, but those with high concentrations of capsaicin can bring tears to the eyes or cause sweating. The current Guinness World Record holder is 'Smokin' Ed's Carolina Reaper' – which is more than 100 times hotter than a jalapeno!

TASTY CHIVES

Chives are an essential kitchen herb, whose pungent leaves with a mild oniony taste are delicious when snipped up finely and added to a salad or to hot dishes – they work particularly well with potatoes, eggs and soft cheese. Even the flowers are edible and make an attractive garnish.

Mature plants are readily available, but this perennial is so easy to start from seed, which gives you the opportunity to grow a named variety and try different types. Sow a few seeds thinly in a small pot and place in a heated propagator. When the seedlings are large enough – in late spring or early summer – divide the rootball into several pieces. Plant in groups of three, spaced about 20cm apart, in a sunny or slightly shaded spot, or in pots filled with soil-based compost. 'Fine Leaved' has a milder flavour than common chives and thinner leaves, while 'Black Isle Blush' boasts showier, light mauve flowers with a deep pink centre. 'Forescate' has slightly garlic-flavoured leaves and pale pink flowers.

DID YOU KNOW?

Chives are the only member of the onion family that are native to both the Old and New World: Europe, Asia and North America.

KALE

Tough, attractive and providing tasty pickings, kale has a lot going for it. It was traditionally grown in rows, but the ornamental looks of some varieties have seen it promoted to the flower garden. Due to its tolerance of cold weather, it will provide interest in beds and borders over winter and into spring.

DID YOU KNOW?

The variety 'Jersey Kale' is renowned for its straight stems that have been known to reach over 5m in height. It used to be grown very successfully in the Channel Islands, where islanders used to dry the stems and sell them as walking sticks to tourists.

Starting indoors

Seeds can be sown in small pots and covered with 2cm of compost. They should germinate within a week. Give seedlings their own pots when large enough to handle. Plant outdoors from late spring to midsummer. If you forget to sow seeds, plug plants are readily available in late spring. Space plants 45cm apart, with 45cm between rows. Firm in place by pressing down with your fingertips so they make good contact with the soil.

FOODIE FAVOURITE

Foodies have fallen in love with black Tuscan kale in recent years, but it has been in Italian kitchens since the eighteenth century. Also known as Cavolo Nero, Nero de Toscana and Lacinato kale, it's a traditional ingredient of minestrone soup and ribollita, a hearty Tuscan stew. The plant makes a statuesque clump of upright, 1m tall, narrow, dark green crinkled leaves.

Looking after plants

Keep well watered, especially over summer, and remove any weeds. As kale grows taller check regularly and refirm in the ground if loosened by wind. Harvest in winter by cutting leaves from the centre of the crown, to encourage more leaves to grow. Stop harvesting when the plants flower, as the leaves turn bitter.

TOP TIP

Kale resents having its roots disturbed. When moving seedlings into their own pots, keep as much compost on the roots as possible.

Troubleshooting

Kale is part of the brassica family, so it is at risk from club root disease. Avoid this by following a crop-rotation programme.

TASTY VARIETIES TO TRY...

- **Starbor F1** – compact, great for windy gardens.
- **Scarlet** – curly, bright violet-green leaves.
- **Redbor F1** – frilly red-tinged leaves.
- **Red Russian F1** – frilly green leaves with red/purple veins.
- **Fizz** – deeply lobed leaves, good for salads when young and cooking when mature.

CULTURE VULTURE

Many Germans celebrate Grühnkohlfahrt, an annual winter event, where partygoers drink schnapps and eat dishes of kale.

TOMATOES

There are thousands of different varieties of tomato you can grow, with fruit that come in many different shapes, colours and sizes, from those as small as grapes to whoppers as large as a tennis ball. To enjoy your own mouthwatering tomatoes, start by sowing seeds indoors. The vigorous seedlings will be ready for planting outdoors in late spring and will reward you with masses of fruit from midsummer onwards.

A host of different fruit

There are thought to be over 5000 different varieties of tomato in the world, whose fruit are generally divided into four main types: cherry, plum, beefsteak and classic round tomatoes. However, some plants have fruit that aren't so easily categorised – such as banana-shaped 'Green Sausage' and pear-shaped 'Red Fig'. Fruit can come in many shades of red, orange, green, yellow and purple, while some are streaked or marked with another shade to give a two-tone effect.

How plants are classified

Most tomato plants are known as *indeterminate* or *cordon* varieties. They are grown as a single-stemmed plant, whose eventual height is controlled by pruning. Ideal in containers or planted in the ground, their growing tips are generally removed when they reach 1.8m and have four trusses of fruit.

Determinate or *bush* tomatoes generally grow to a fixed height and spread. They produce lots of shoots and can form sprawling plants that need lots of room, so are best planted in the ground.

Dwarf or *miniature* tomatoes are extremely compact. They contain a gene that restricts their growth and are ideal for pots or even hanging baskets.

Semi-determinate tomatoes are similar to cordon tomatoes, but don't grow as tall.

Sowing seeds

Sow a few seeds in pots filled with seed compost and cover with a thin layer of vermiculite. Water and pop in a label – this is most important if you're growing more than one variety. Place in a heated propagator and remove once the seeds have germinated, usually after 7–10 days. Keep the compost damp and once seedlings are about 2.5cm tall, prick out into individual pots. At the end of May plant in a sunny spot or move into larger containers – a single cordon tomato is suitable for a 30cm pot, or plant three in a growing bag.

Growing tips

Tomatoes aren't difficult to grow, but they do need some attention to ensure you get a bumper crop.

- Remove the side-shoots that form in the leaf joints of cordon tomatoes when they are about 3cm long – they should snap out with a swift downwards movement.
- Feed weekly with liquid tomato food once flowers appear.
- Ensure the pots never dry out. Irregular watering can result in black hard patches forming on the bottom of fruit. Known as blossom end rot, this is caused by a lack of calcium, which is found in water.
- When the first truss of tiny tomatoes appears on cordon varieties, strip the leaves away from under it to allow light and air to reach the fruit.
- Allow cordon varieties to produce four sets of flowering trusses, then pinch out the growing tip to ensure all of the plant's energy goes into producing fruit and not making more foliage.

DID YOU KNOW?

Tomatoes were considered an aphrodisiac in France and were
known as *pomme d'amour*, or love apples.

CULTURE VULTURE

Each year in August, around 20,000 people take part in La
Tomatina, a tomato-throwing festival in the Spanish city of
Buñol. Over 100 tons of overripe tomatoes are thrown by
participants in this massive food fight.

A little bit of history

Tomatoes are native to parts of South and Central America and
are believed to have been first grown by the Aztecs and Mayans
in around 500AD. No one knows exactly when they arrived in
Europe, but some historians believe seeds were brought back by
Spanish conquistadors in the sixteenth century. These original
plants bore little resemblance to the tomatoes we eat today
– the fruit were small and yellow, and plants were treated as
ornamental climbers rather than vegetables.

Tomatoes arrived in Britain in the 1590s. They were treated
with contempt – the fruit were thought to be poisonous and
respected herbalist John Gerard considered them 'ranke
and stinking'. In fact, tomatoes are related to such poisonous
plants as henbane, hemlock and deadly nightshade! By the
mid-eighteenth century, tomatoes were widely eaten by the
population and plant breeding really took off in the nineteenth
and twentieth centuries, leading to the introduction of new
varieties – now described as heirloom or heritage varieties.

Some of these old-timers are still available to grow, but today modern varieties tend to have better disease resistance or produce greater yields than their forebears.

10 HEIRLOOM TOMATOES WORTH TRYING

1 Red Cherry 1877
2 German Pink 1883
3 Brandywine 1889
4 Golden Sunrise 1890s
5 Ailsa Craig 1912
6 Sioux 1944
7 Big Boy F1 1949
8 Gardener's Delight AGM 1950
9 Roma VF 1955
10 Evergreen 1956

PEAS

Freshly picked peas are a taste sensation and are so much better than anything bought from a shop. The reason? The moment peas are harvested, their sugars start to turn to starch and the flavour is impaired. This truly is one of the vegetables that is best picked moments before cooking to get them at their best.

When to sow

Many varieties are suitable for sowing outdoors from early March, if the conditions are right. Temperatures need to be around 10°C and soil shouldn't be too wet or cold. Wait until later in the month or into April if the weather isn't warm enough. Some varieties are suitable for sowing up until midsummer to provide a succession of fresh pods.

Sowing seeds

Choose a sunny, well-drained spot and work in plenty of well-rotted manure or garden compost before sowing to improve the soil. Make a shallow trench, 23cm wide by 5cm deep, and sow in two parallel lines, spacing seeds 5cm apart. Cover with soil and water in well. If you've got a small garden, try sowing into large pots filled with multi-purpose compost. Make holes with a dibber, 5cm deep, every 5cm and drop a seed in. Cover with soil and water in.

Supporting act

When seedlings are about 5cm tall, add some supports to prevent them collapsing under their own weight. Either place twigs into the ground at regular intervals or place bamboo canes along the row and attach a sheet of support netting for them to clamber up. If growing in pots, either push in twigs or construct a wigwam structure.

Aftercare

Make sure that the soil or compost is kept damp in dry spells. Peas will generally be ready for picking about three months after sowing. Ensure a steady supply by picking regularly while small and tender to encourage more pods to develop – those at the bottom of the plants will generally be the first to mature.

PERFECT PEAS TO TRY

- **Kelvedon Wonder** – compact, with heavy crops.
- **Blauwschokker** – attractive, dusky purple pods.
- **Hurst Green Shaft** – sweet-tasting and vigorous.
- **Canoe** – long, curved pods.
- **Feltham First** – compact, popular old variety.

Sowing in guttering

There's a clever way of starting peas that's perfect if the conditions aren't suitable outdoors this month. Track down a length of old plastic guttering and drill a few drainage holes in the base. Half-fill with multi-purpose compost, then sow seeds in two staggered rows, 5cm apart. Water and keep under cover until the seedlings are about 10cm tall. Dig a shallow trench outdoors and carefully slide out the contents of the guttering, then firm the compost in place and water.

CULTURE VULTURE

Peas were the favourite vegetable of Thomas Jefferson, the third president of the United States. He grew 15 different varieties of English pea in his kitchen garden at Monticello, in Virginia.

DID YOU KNOW?

In the nineteenth and early twentieth centuries, pea seeds were found among the contents of tombs explored by archaeologists in Egypt. So-called 'mummy peas' became a popular souvenir. According to records, in 1922, when Howard Carter found the tomb of Tutankhamun, he discovered seven pea seeds among the artefacts and over the next few decades, many claimed to have raised crops grown from these peas. However, scientists at the Royal Botanic Gardens at Kew have dashed this tale – it is highly unlikely the seeds would be viable after 3000 years.

HOW TO PREPARE A SEEDBED

Before you sow seeds or plant vegetables in early spring, you need to give the soil some attention. Seeds are unlikely to germinate and plants will struggle to grow in soil that hasn't been cultivated sufficiently.

The best time to do this is in late winter or early spring, to ground that was dug in autumn – if you didn't get round to digging the soil in autumn, don't worry, you're just going to have to put a bit more elbow grease into preparing it now.

Use a fork to break up any large lumps of soil and roughly level the surface – removing any stones that work their way up. Rake the soil backwards and forwards in one direction until the clods have all gone and the soil has a fine, even finish – draw soil into hollows and break down any mounds. Then rake in another direction, 90 degrees to the first. You want a flat and even surface, where the texture of the soil resembles breadcrumbs.

If you decide to do this in the winter or if the weather is cold, cover the prepared surface with a cloche. This will keep the soil warm and enable you to sow and plant earlier outdoors.

CAULIFLOWERS

Caulis can cost a bomb in the shops, especially if you go for some of the more unusual coloured ones, so it's worth considering growing your own if you want to save a packet. However, this isn't a crop to start growing without some careful thought – it can take up to year before they are ready for harvesting and caulis require plenty of space, making it a vegetable that's probably better suited to an allotment than the back garden.

Sowing seeds

The easiest way to sow cauliflower seeds is in modular trays filled with seed compost. Sow a couple of seeds in each cell, 1cm deep. Water and place in a light spot. After germination remove the weaker of each seedling. Keep indoors until midsummer, then gradually acclimatise them to life outdoors over a ten-day period. Ideally, place them in a cold frame. If you don't have one, place them in a sheltered spot outdoors.

Planting out

The young caulis can be planted out in early summer. Make sure the ground has been well prepared, but is firmer than a normal seedbed. As cauliflowers are a member of the brassica family, ensure they don't go into ground that has been used for any of their relatives over the last three years. Plant summer-cropping varieties 60cm apart, with 60cm between rows, autumn- and winter-cropping types 75cm apart.

Routine care

Ensure that plants never dry out and keep a close eye out for hungry caterpillars and birds. The caulis will be ready for harvesting from late summer to early winter, depending on the variety – cut the heads while they're still firm and compact.

Cauliflower heads will discolour if exposed to too
much sunlight. Protect them with their own foliage
when they're about the size of an egg; snap the
midribs of a few outer leaves and fold them over the
heads. If they don't stay in place, make a few holes
through them and thread together with twine.

A RANGE OF COLOURS

Cauliflowers come in a range of colours. If you want a
traditional white variety, go for dependable 'All The Year
Round'. 'Romanesco' has lime-green, conical heads, while
'Graffiti' F1 boasts purple heads.

A little bit of history

A member of the cabbage family, cauliflowers are thought to
originate from Asia Minor. They were first mentioned as far
back as the sixth century BC, although they didn't arrive in
Britain until the sixteenth century. In 1586, they were known as
Cyprus Coleworts, possibly because the first cauliflowers were
transported from the Mediterranean island to this country.
Eleven years later, botanist John Gerard referred to them as
Cole flower in his famous book *The Herball*.

' A cauliflower is nothing but a cabbage with a college
education.' Mark Twain.

GROWING ONIONS FROM SETS

Onions may be fairly inexpensive to buy, but growing your own allows you to try scores of differently named varieties that look and taste different. They can be raised from seed, but it's far easier to start them off as sets – small, baby bulbs. It is possible to plant onions in large containers, although you would need to plant up a lot of pots to produce a worthwhile crop, so it's far better to plant them 10cm apart in a sunny patch of soil, leaving 30cm between rows. Planting is a doddle. Make a hole with a dibber and simply drop the bulb in, tips pointing up. Replace the soil, making sure the tip is just peeking above the surface. The bulbs will be ready for harvesting in summer, when the leaves sag and turn brown. After lifting, let them dry out on a wire or wooden rack for three weeks before storing in a cool, dry and dark place.

VARIETIES TO TRY

- **Red Baron** – red onion with a strong flavour.
- **Rossa lunga di Firenze** – a torpedo-shaped onion from Italy.
- **Sturon** – large bulbs that keep for ages in storage.
- **Hercules AGM** – large, round, juicy bulbs with golden-brown skins.
- **Stuttgarter Stanfield** – flattish, yellow-skinned bulbs, with a mild flavour.

Plants can sometimes bolt or run
to seed prematurely, so nip out
any flower shoots that appear
and make sure the plants are
kept moist in dry weather.

How to make a traditional onion rope

A traditional way of storing onions is to braid them into ropes. Not only does it look attractive, but it also allows air to circulate around the bulbs to reduce the risk of the crop being damaged by fungal diseases. Cut a 60cm length of brown twine, then gather three bulbs together and make a firm knot with the twine just above their necks. Wind the foliage around the twine, keeping it upright. Add more bulbs, letting them rest on those below and winding the foliage upwards along the twine, tying in each group of onions as you go. When you run out of space, tie a knot around the onions at the top with more twine. Use the tops of the foliage to form a loop and hang the rope in a cool, dry place. Bulbs can be snipped off the rope when needed.

GROWING IN POTS

In the past, it was believed that you needed a dedicated vegetable patch or allotment to grow vegetables, but the realisation that many edibles could be grown in containers has meant that even those with tiny plots can grow their own crops. Plastic, stone, terracotta, metal and just about any other type of container are fine for edibles. Recycled containers look good; ask your local deli for some used olive-oil drums or root around in a skip and see what you can reuse. Most crops need a container that is 30–45cm wide, although more compact plants, like some herbs, will do well in much smaller pots. Make sure whatever you use is large enough for your chosen plants to grow comfortably – if it's a tight fit, they're unlikely to do well. Most annual crops will do well in multi-purpose compost, which contains enough nutrients to give them a kick-start; perennial vegetables and herbs are better in a soil-based compost.

10 GOOD VEGETABLES FOR POTS

1 Aubergine
2 Beetroot
3 Carrots
4 Courgette
5 French beans
6 Peppers (sweet and chilli)
7 Potatoes
8 Radish
9 Salad leaves
10 Tomatoes

'The secret of good veg growing is to put in time little and often, so you keep on top of weeds and any problem pests and diseases. You can't "catch up" all in one frantic weekend, just before you expect to be picking, because the odds are that your veg will have vanished by then.'

Alan Titchmarsh, *The Complete How To Be a Gardener*

This month brings real optimism, seemingly shaking off the last remnants of winter and trying to push us forwards into spring. At this time of year, our gardens truly sparkle with life: the plump shoots of perennials nose their way above the soil before romping away with gusto; beds are enlivened by a multitude of flowering bulbs; and clouds of pretty blossom fleetingly decorate the branches of trees before being replaced by a mass of unfurling emerald leaves. Now, finally, it is safe to say that spring has well and truly sprung.

It's not just our plants that seem to have woken up. The garden has become a hive of activity as bees flit from flower to flower, on the search for nectar, while ladybirds and other insects appear like magic during a sunny spell. Even birds are noisier and more industrious as they seek out suitable nesting sites. Unfortunately, not all creatures that pop up are beneficial, because now aphids and other pests are also on the march, so it pays to check plants regularly to prevent problems getting out of hand.

Under cover, pots of seedlings are fighting for elbow room on windowsills, greenhouse benches and conservatory floors, while many gardeners are preparing for the next lot of sowings, with an army of seed packets lined up in date order ready to be sown outside. Don't be lulled into a false sense of spring too early, though, and try not to be hasty to get everything in at once; take your local weather conditions and climate into account and sow a little later if necessary. If you do go ahead, remember that overnight frosts are always to be expected in April, so keep an eye on the weather forecast and be prepared to cover vulnerable plants with sheets of fleece or cloches.

Square foot gardening

If your garden is small but you want to join in the grow-your-own revolution, try this method of growing vegetables. In the 1970s Mel Bartholomew in the USA noticed that many gardeners lacked growing space, so he came up with the idea of making a 3ft by 3ft wooden bed which was divided into nine individual squares by a wooden grid fixed to the top. This bed could then be placed on a patio, lawn, deck or another part of the garden permanently or just for the duration of the growing season. After filling it with compost, nine different crops can be grown in the planting squares. Due to the confined space, it's best to pick compact veggies to grow, such as peppers, beetroot, salad leaves, spring onions and radishes.

BEETROOT

If you've only ever eaten beetroot from a jar you don't know what you're missing – fresh roots have a warm, earthy taste that's far superior to those soggy slices drenched in malt vinegar. And they're not all round and purple, beetroot actually come in a wide range of colours, shapes and sizes.

Seeds can be sown outdoors any time between mid-April and late June – earlier than this and they'll need protecting with cloches. Prepare the soil well, adding in multi-purpose compost or well-rotted manure, then make 3cm-deep trenches in the ground and 'station sow' to ensure you get a good crop – this means sowing two seeds every 10cm and thinning them later to one seedling. Don't waste the removed seedlings – the young leaves can be cooked and eaten like spinach.

FOODIE FACT

Australians are the biggest consumers of beetroot per capita in the world. Even fast-food chains serve burgers with slices of the vegetable inside the bun.

IS IT A SEED?

Each beetroot seed is a cluster of up to six seeds contained within a dried fruit case. This case contains a natural seed germination inhibitor that can be removed by soaking the corky cluster in warm water for about 30 minutes before sowing.

Another option is to grow beetroot in large pots filled with multi-purpose compost. Sow seeds thinly across the surface and cover with a 3cm layer of finely sifted compost. Thin out seedlings, leaving about 10cm between plants to ensure there's plenty of room for the roots to swell.

Keep the area free from weeds. Do water regularly – not only does it help roots swell to full size, it also prevents them splitting and reduces the likelihood of them running to seed early. Most globe-shaped beetroots should be ready to harvest in 11 weeks, while longer varieties take closer to four months.

IF YOU LIKE BEETROOT, TRY THESE...

- **Red Ace F1** – round, dark purple roots. Resistant to dry conditions.
- **Chioggia** – pink roots that reveal dark red and white concentric rings when sliced.
- **Cylindra** – long, dark pink roots that are perfect for slicing.
- **Boltardy** – spherical roots with a smooth skin. Popular due to its resistance to bolting.
- **Burpee's Golden** – a US introduction in the 1940s, it has golden skin and orange flesh.

A little bit of history

Beetroot is thought to have evolved from sea beet, a plant native to the shores of Europe, North Africa and southern Asia. It was originally domesticated in parts of the eastern Mediterranean and Middle East, and was esteemed by the ancient Greeks. Beetroot was mentioned in English cookbooks dating back to the fourteenth century, but back then the roots were long and slim. The globular roots that we know now didn't make an appearance until the sixteenth century.

SQUASH AND PUMPKINS

There are hundreds of different pumpkins and squash varieties in myriad shapes, colours and sizes. They are divided into two groups: summer squashes are harvested from June to September and need to be eaten within days of picking, while pumpkins and winter squash are ready in early autumn and can be eaten immediately or stored for up to three months.

Seeds should be started off indoors – sow two seeds, 2.5cm deep, in 8cm pots filled with multi-purpose compost. Pop into a heated propagator. Remove the weakest of the pair after germination. Young plants will grow quickly and are ready to go outdoors once the danger of frost has passed in late May or early June – they prefer a sunny spot with moisture-retentive soil improved with garden compost or manure. Another option is to plant them into 30cm pots.

The traditional way of growing pumpkins and squashes is to allow stems to trail along the ground, but varieties with smaller fruit can be trained up sturdy supports to maximise growing space. A wigwam made with chunky canes or poles will hold the weight of medium-sized pumpkins, and can be placed among ornamental plants to add vertical interest to a border. Those whose gardens are tight for space can train growing plants against walls, fences and trellis, or over pergolas and arches.

HEAVYWEIGHT CHAMPION

At the 2012 New England Giant Pumpkin Weigh-Off in Massachusetts, an 'Atlantic Giant' pumpkin weighing 911.27kg was crowned heaviest in the world by Guinness World Records.

Try these summer squash

Patty pans are flying-saucer-shaped squash with scalloped edges – the F1 varieties white-skinned 'Polo', golden-yellow 'Sunburst' and 'Total Eclipse', a dark green variety with white spots, are all worth growing. A group of summer squash known as crooknecks have slender, U-shaped fruit that look unusual in a veg bed. 'Summer Crookneck' has bright yellow, knobbly-skinned curved fruit, while 'Early Golden Crookneck' boasts club-shaped, golden-yellow fruit. 'Rolet' is a dark-green-skinned squash with round fruit the size of a cricket ball.

Or these winter pumpkins and squash

'Turk's Turban' is a distinctive squash with bright orange, hat-shaped fruit that are flecked with red, white and green markings. 'Blue Banana' boasts 60-cm long blue fruit that resemble a Zeppelin, while 'Baby Bear' and 'Jack Be Little' are small and orange. Bright-yellow 'Hasta La Pasta' F1 can be roasted whole and has stringy flesh that can be eaten like pasta. 'Crown Prince' F1 is a pumpkin with squat fruit that have distinctive grey, ribbed skin and bright orange flesh.

TOP TIP

When sowing, place seeds vertically, not flat – this prevents moisture on the surface, which leads to rotting.

A little bit of history

Pumpkins and squash are both members of the curcubita family, a group of vegetables that includes melons, courgettes and cucumbers. They are thought to have originated in North America and seeds have been found in Mexico that are believed to date back to 7000BC. Native Americans domesticated pumpkins and relied on them to get them through harsh winters. Apart from eating the flesh, they used the pumpkin in many ingenious ways. Seeds were crushed into powder to use as medicine, the shell was divided into two to form bowls, while the skin was sometimes dried, cut into strips and woven together to form mats. It's believed that pumpkins were brought to Europe in the fifteenth century by explorer Christopher Columbus.

IT'S A FACT
Pumpkins are 90 per cent water!

COOL DOWN GREENHOUSES

Now the weather is improving, shade greenhouse glass to prevent temperatures building up too much inside and to safeguard seedlings from the scorching rays of the sun. Either install netting on the inside of the glass or paint the outside of the panes with white shade paint – this may need reapplying over the summer if it is particularly wet. On hot days, make sure you open the vents and doors to the greenhouse, and splash the floor and staging in the morning and afternoon with water to cool the air and create a humid atmosphere. Remember to close all the vents and doors in the evening if cooler temperatures are predicted.

COOL CUCUMBERS

You don't need many cucumber plants to keep you supplied with tasty fruit throughout the summer. A single plant can produce around 15 cucumbers if properly cared for, so a couple of plants would probably be enough for an average family, unless you are really passionate about eating them.

Indoor and outdoor cucumbers

There are two main types of cucumber: indoor types are suited to growing in unheated greenhouses and are F1 cultivars that produce high-quality, long, smooth fruit similar to those found in the supermarket. The indoor varieties produce both male and female flowers, so the male flowers need removing to prevent the female flowers being cross pollinated, which would give bitter-tasting fruit. Varieties with all-female flowers are also available.

Outdoor cucumbers are sometimes labelled ridge cucumbers and this group includes many heritage varieties. The fruit is generally smaller with rougher skin. Plants produce male and female flowers, but no flowers should be removed as they are required by pollinating insects, which need both sets of flowers to be present. Outdoor types can also be grown under cover.

TOP TIP

It's easy to tell male and female flowers apart: female flowers have a baby fruit growing behind them, while male flowers have a plain stalk.

Starting from seed

Sow two seeds on their side, 1.5cm deep, in pots. Remove the weakest of the seedlings after germination. Keep the young plants in a warm place until late spring, then plant out into the ground or into pots outdoors or in an unheated greenhouse.

Growing them

Outdoor cucumbers can be allowed to sprawl over the ground or can be trained up supports. In small gardens, plant two cucumbers in a growing bag and tie the main stem of each to bamboo canes.

If you are growing in a greenhouse and don't have a border of soil, plant them into growing bags. Tie the shoots to a cane or wire and train the growth vertically towards the roof. Once the stem has reached the top of the greenhouse, remove the growing tip.

To ensure cucumber plants put all their energy into producing good-quality fruit, pinch out the tips of side shoots two leaves beyond a female flower and pinch out the tips of flowerless side shoots once they are 60cm long.

DID YOU KNOW?

Cucumbers contain no saturated fat or cholesterol and 100g of the vegetable contains just 16 calories.

IT'S A FACT

The phrase 'as cool as a cucumber' was first recorded in 1732, in John Gay's *A New Song of New Similies*.

Best fruit

Keep plants happy by feeding them every 10–14 days with a balanced liquid fertiliser, changing this to a high-potash feed once the first fruits start to set. Cucumbers will thrive if you keep the humidity high within the greenhouse by watering the floor in the morning during sunny weather.

5

THE BEST CUCUMBERS TO TRY

1 **Tiffany F1**
Long, dark fruit for growing indoors.

2 **Melonie**
Indoor cucumber with unusual striped fruit.

3 **Tasty King F1**
Very long fruit. Good indoors or outside.

4 **Crystal Lemon**
Lemon-shaped yellow fruit for growing outdoors.

5 **Bush Champion**
Outdoor type that's good in pots.

RADISHES

Few salad vegetables are as easy or as quick to grow as radishes. Seeds can be sown any time from March until the end of the summer, and will generally be ready for harvesting within eight weeks. Ideal in sun or partial shade, radishes can be grown in pots, raised beds or used to fill in empty spaces in your beds or borders. There are many varieties available in different colours, shapes and sizes; longer-rooted ones are best in the ground, but short-rooted varieties are great in pots – round ones can even be raised in windowboxes or other shallow containers. Sow 1cm deep and thin to around 3cm apart, when seedlings are large enough to handle. Leave 15cm between rows. Looking after them is a doddle; keep plants well watered, especially during periods of dry weather, and remove any weeds that appear around them. Radishes will be ready for harvesting in five–eight weeks – don't leave them in the ground too long or the roots will become large, woody and taste far too strong. Pick what you need, taking care not to disturb remaining ones.

A host of varieties

There are lots of brilliant radishes to grow. 'Sparkler' has deep scarlet and white roots, while 'Amethyst' boasts round purple roots and crisp white flesh. Both are good in small pots. 'French Breakfast' is a mild-tasting radish with cylindrical roots. For something really different, try 'Hilds Blauer Herbst und Winter' – its long purple roots can be picked as late as November.

TOP TIP

If you're growing in pots, don't be stingy. For a worthwhile crop, choose a container that is at least 30cm diameter and 20cm deep.

AUTHENTIC SALSA

A proper Mexican salsa is made using tomatillos, a tomato-like fruit that develops inside a papery husk. These little fruits are blitzed together with chilli peppers, coriander, lime juice and onion to make the fiery sauce. Tomatillos are available from specialist food shops, but you're unlikely to find them in an average supermarket. Fortunately, they're really easy to grow from seeds – green, purple and yellow varieties are available. They'll grow quickly to form a bushy plant that's smothered in large yellow flowers prior to the berries forming. These will be ready to harvest in late summer, when they are fully swollen and the papery husk starts to split. Tomatillos are tender, so start them off indoors and move outdoors in early summer. Grow in a sunny sheltered spot and water regularly. Plants will need supporting with a cane to prevent the brittle stems collapsing.

RUNNER BEANS

A traditional favourite that produces masses of long, flat pods over an extended period, runner beans are usually ready to harvest 12 weeks or so after sowing. There are many varieties worth trying. 'St George' has red and white flowers followed by 30cm-long, smooth pods, while 'Lady Di' has heavy crops of long, slender beans. 'Celebration' has pink flowers that appear before its long pods and 'Wisley Magic' boasts red flowers and 35cm-long pods.

Supporting beans

The traditional method for growing runner beans on allotments and vegetable patches is to construct a beanpole – a double row of bamboo canes held together by a crossbar. To make one, mark out two straight lines, 60cm apart. Then push 2.4m-long canes, 60cm apart, along the length of the first row. Repeat along the second row, making sure the canes are directly opposite those in the first row. Angle the canes towards each other until they just overlap. Secure the tops by using another cane as a crossbar and tie together securely.

Another option is to make a strong wigwam of canes. These are far more ornamental, so are better suited to beds, borders and raised beds. Simply space four to eight canes 15–22cm apart in a circle and bind the tops together with twine.

Sowing and growing

Make a 5cm-deep hole at the foot of each support and drop in two seeds. Cover and water. After germination, remove the weakest of the pair of seedlings and allow the other to climb upwards. To help it, you can secure it to the cane with twine.

Water beans frugally in dull weather or while they are establishing, increasing the amount you give them after the first flower buds appear and until the last of the pods has been picked. Mulch the surface of the soil with garden compost or well-rotted manure to help lock in moisture and prevent weeds from growing.

Harvesting

When beans reach the top of their supports, pinch out the tops to encourage more pods. Snip off pods with a pair of scissors when they are large enough to eat. Harvest every two to three days to ensure a constant supply and to prevent those left on the plant turning tough.

DID YOU KNOW?

The stems of most climbing beans move upwards in anti-clockwise fashion but runner bean stems twine clockwise.

Growing in pots

If you've got a small garden, try growing a dwarf runner bean in a pot. 'Hestia' grows to just 45cm tall, its showy red and white flowers are followed by masses of succulent beans. 'Pickwick' has even heavier yields of 25cm-long pods. Plant into pots that are at least 45cm wide and fill with a 50/50 mixture of soil-based compost and multi-purpose compost. Construct a wigwam of canes in the pot and sow seeds at the base of each support.

A little bit of history

Runner beans are thought to have originated in Mexico, arriving in Britain during the seventeenth century. They are believed to have been introduced by John Tradescant the Elder, a plant collector and gardener to Charles I. Originally used as ornamental climbers due to their colourful flowers, it wasn't until the eighteenth century that the beans were eaten. Philip Miller, keeper of Chelsea Physic Garden from 1721 to 1770, is credited with being the first person in this country to cook them.

 ## BASIL

Shop-bought plants tend to be multi-sown with lots of seedlings packed into a small pot. Lack of space means these pots soon run out of steam, but if you grow your own basil it's possible to grow stronger plants that will provide leaves all summer long.

Start by sowing a few seeds on the surface of a small pot – most will germinate, so only sow a few more than you need. Cover the seeds with a fine layer of vermiculite and place in a heated windowsill propagator.

The seeds should germinate within a week. When the seedlings are large enough to handle, transfer each to a small pot. Plants will grow quickly, so move them into a slightly larger pot every time you notice roots poking through the drainage holes. Pinch back the growing tips to encourage bushy growth.

Plants can be moved outdoors in late spring or early summer, or keep them on a windowsill indoors, where they'll always be close at hand. Water them regularly to prevent a check to growth – basil plants hate having cold, wet roots, so always water plants in the morning, not in the evening.

---

5 GOOD BASIL TYPES TO TRY

1 **Purple Ruffles**
Heavily fringed, showy dark purple leaves.

2 **Genovese**
Large, bright green, sweet leaves that are delcious with mozzarella and tomatoes.

3 **Cinnamon**
Bushy plant with aromatic red-veined green leaves.

4 **Napoletano**
Huge, green aromatic leaves.

5 **Siam Queen**
Tasty, slightly hairy oval leaves; great in Thai cooking.

A little bit of history

Although it's often associated with Italian cuisine, basil is actually native to India and other tropical regions of Asia. A variety known as holy basil (*Ocimum tenuiflorum*) is considered sacred to Hindus and is grown outside temples and homes. Followers believe it guards against misfortunes and represents purity, harmony and serenity.

Basil arrived in Britain in the 1500s. At the time, its foliage was dried and powdered to make snuff, which was inhaled to cure colds, headaches and other ailments. Few thought the leaves worth eating and the plant was viewed with deep mistrust. John Gerard, the leading botanist and author of the influential *The Herball*, reckoned that if you spat out the leaves onto the ground, worms would spontaneously appear.

Basil didn't become a mainstay of our kitchens until the latter part of the twentieth century. Today, there are around 50 different varieties that are available to grow from seed in the UK.

Authentic pesto sauce

Basil is most famous as the main ingredient of pesto, a sauce that also includes pine nuts, garlic, Parmesan and olive oil. The fragrant sauce originated in Liguria, north-west Italy in the 1860s. To make an authentic pesto, use 'Tigullio', a variety with slightly curled leaves that is widely grown in this coastal region.

WATCH OUT FOR APHIDS

If you spot aphids early you can prevent a potential problem getting out of hand, but if ignored the results can be devastating. An infestation of these sap-suckers will result in deformed leaves and stems, and will usually affect the quality and quantity of what you are hoping to harvest in a few months' time.

There are around 500 different species of aphid in Britain – not all attack vegetables, but plenty do. A few isolated aphids on bushy vegetable plants can be rubbed off with your fingers, but denser populations gathering around the tops of shoots will require tougher treatment, so remove the tip, along with the unwanted pests, by pinching back to a pair of healthy buds. Although you may not want to, it will result in bushier specimens as it will encourage plants to produce side shoots.

Pinching back is fine if the aphids are only occupying a few shoots, but if they're under leaves or on many branches, you might need to spray the plants. There are lots of ready-to-use organic pesticides, or for a chemical alternative, try using a fatty acid concentrate, which has the same consistency as liquid soap.

'Nature moves, gardens evolve, everything changes. I have never understood gardens that try to stay the same, where constant perfection and perpetual flowering are the goals. I like the lulls, the anticipation that comes with waiting for the next moment.'

Alys Fowler, *The Edible Garden*

A bridge between spring and summer, May is a month that many gardeners never want to end. The garden is full of life; pollinating insects might be spotted flitting between flowers, while early perennials are in bloom in our beds and borders. Many deciduous trees and shrubs, now fully clothed in their verdant livery, are in full flower.

It's a time when there's much to do in the vegetable garden. Beetroot, carrots, radishes, peas and a host of other crops can now be sown outdoors – but a word of caution, May can be a funny month. Although the days are generally lighter and warmer, often the month can be cold and wet, and frosts are still a cause for concern for some – in these areas, seeds sown too early will result in seedlings that are vulnerable to a sharp overnight frost.

Finally, now you can reclaim your windowsills, greenhouse benches and other germinating spots indoors, all the places where tender vegetables have been lovingly nurtured for the last few months. As the outside temperatures start to rise by the end of May and late frosts become more unlikely, these plants can be transferred to sunny spots outdoors. To be on the safe side, though, be prepared to move them if the weather does take a turn for the worse, or to cover them in a layer of protective fleece.

The improvement in the conditions outdoors doesn't just benefit our vegetables though, unfortunately annual weeds absolutely love it too and will be popping up everywhere. Be vigilant. If you've got a small garden, pull them up by hand whenever you spy one. Those with larger plots might find it easier to put a set amount of time aside each week to keep on top of the weeding.

SWEETCORN

Sweetcorn needs a fair amount of space to grow, but it's one of the most rewarding crops you can cultivate. Fresh cobs taste much better than anything you can buy – the sugar in the kernels starts turning to starch the moment the cobs have been picked, so the sooner you eat them, the better. There's no telling when cobs in the shops were picked, but it probably explains why sometimes they can be pretty tasteless.

Sowing seeds

It's possible to start seeds in small pots indoors and then plant them outside. However, they hate having their roots disturbed and germinate readily, so it's just as easy to sow them directly into the ground. Drop two seeds into the bottom of 2.5cm deep holes, spaced 35cm apart. Cover and water. Remove the weakest of each pair of seedlings when they are about 2cm tall. Remember that each plant will produce one to two cobs, so work out how many you want before sowing.

Looking after them

Keep well watered, especially during dry periods. In addition to its normal roots, sweetcorn produces roots from its lower stem above the ground. Known as adventitious roots, these are easy to damage when you are weeding around plants with a Dutch hoe. Protect these more exposed roots and give plants more stability by mounding up soil around them with a draw hoe.

When to pick

Cobs are generally ready for harvesting when the silky tassels at the ends turn brown. Check by peeling back some leaves and stabbing a kernel with a fingernail. If the juice that oozes out is milky, they're ready to pick. To remove, simply twist the cob away from the plant.

5 SWEETCORN TO TRY

1 **Indian Summer F1**
   Cobs with yellow, red, white and purple kernels.
2 **Swift F1**
   Extra-sweet golden-yellow kernels.
3 **Mirai F1**
   Creamy yellow kernels.
4 **Lark F1**
   Very soft, sweet yellow kernels.
5 **Ambrosia F1**
   Yellow and creamy white kernels.

The three sisters

This is a traditional technique for growing vegetables that was originally practised by Native Americans. The Iroquois and other tribes believed that sweetcorn, climbing beans and squash were like three inseparable sisters that would only thrive when grown in close proximity. Essentially a form of companion planting, the tall stems of the sweetcorn provide a support for the beans, while the beans fix nitrogen with their roots to feed the soil the following season. The trailing stems of the squash cover the soil below, preventing weeds from growing and locking in moisture for the three growing plants.

TOP TIP

Sweetcorn is wind pollinated, so plant in large blocks. This way, the male flowers at the top of the plant will be able to shed their pollen onto the female tassels below.

AROMATIC ROSEMARY

There are over 100 different types of rosemary available in the UK. All have strongly flavoured needle-like leaves, but their differences come in terms of their height, shape and the colour of their flowers that appear in spring and early summer.

Rosmarinus officinalis 'Miss Jessopp's Upright' has blue flowers and can grow to 1.5m, while *R. officinalis* Prostratus Group is a sprawling, low-growing plant that's unlikely to exceed 15cm in height. Among the showiest are 'Lady in White', which boasts snowy white flowers on upright branches and 'Majorca Pink', whose arching branches are laden with masses of mauve-pink blooms during May and June.

Where to plant them

Native to the Mediterranean, this is a sun-loving herb that does best when planted in well-drained soil in a sunny sheltered spot – improve clay soil with leafmould or grit prior to planting. If you don't have enough room in a bed, grow plants in 20cm pots filled with soil-based compost.

Plant care

Rosemary is drought tolerant but will need watering regularly during dry spells in summer, especially if they are grown in containers. Feed plants with a balanced fertiliser after they have finished flowering.

The plants require very little pruning. Remove wayward branches or any that spoil the shape of the plant. Keep plants compact by cutting back stems after the blooms start to fade or plants will become leggy.

Leaf-eating pest

Generally trouble free, plants may be attacked by rosemary beetle, a small oval insect marked by metallic green and purple stripes. This pest sticks out like a sore thumb, so keep a close eye on plants and pick off these beetles before they have the chance to strip the stems of their leaves.

GRAFTED VEGETABLES

Over the past few years there's been a steady increase in the number of grafted vegetable plants that are available to gardeners. These are produced by uniting two varieties of the same vegetable to make a single plant. For example, the rootstock of a vigorous wild tomato can be attached to the top of a variety known for its tasty fruit.

The first grafted vegetables appeared in Japan and Korea during the 1920s, when watermelon plants were grafted onto the roots of a squash, as both are members of the curcubit family. Due to the success of the experiment, other vegetables were propagated in the same way and today over 54 per cent of Japan's vegetables are produced by grafted plants. In the UK, 60 per cent of commercial glasshouse tomatoes are grown on grafted plants.

Although they've been used by commercial growers for some time, these plants didn't become widely available to gardeners in Britain until 2008, when five varieties of tomato were sold via a mail-order seed company. Today, there are many different grafted tomatoes available, along with grafted chilli peppers, aubergine, sweet peppers, squash, sweet potato and melon.

Unfortunately, the work involved in propagating these plants means they are significantly more expensive than those grown from seed. However, the nurseries believe this is outweighed by their advantages. They claim that grafted vegetable plants can produce 75 per cent more crops than standard plants because they are stronger, faster growing and more reliable. Due to their robust growth, they are also thought to be better at shrugging off diseases than traditional vegetable plants.

COURGETTES

Courgettes are one of the most productive vegetables you can grow; a single plant can easily produce over twenty fruit, so it's best not to raise too many unless you're a diehard fan. They're one of the easiest plants to grow from seed. Simply plant two, 2.5cm deep in a small pot. Place in a propagator to germinate, then remove the weaker of the two seedlings. When roots poke through the drainage holes in the bottom, move the seedling to a 12cm container. Plant out into the ground in early summer, making sure the leaves have space to spread 45cm in all directions. Another option is to plant into growing bags or 30cm pots filled with multi-purpose compost.

A wealth of varieties

Forget about the anonymous water-filled truncheons available in the shops – there are masses of named varieties you can grow, in many different colours, shapes and sizes. Round varieties are ideal for stuffing. Among the best are 'Rondo di Nizza', a pale green Italian variety and dark green 'Eight Ball'. Orange 'Summer Ball' F1 look wonderful and should be picked when they're the size of a tennis ball.

The fruits of 'Defender' are a traditional shape and dark green colour, while 'Zephyr' F1 boasts slender, creamy yellow tapering fruit with a distinctive pale green tip. 'Bianco di Trieste' has near-white fruit and 'Orelia' F1 has 17cm-long, bright yellow fruit. 'Patio Star' F1 and 'Buckingham' F1 are more compact than most, making them perfect for pots.

Climbing courgette

'Black Forest' is a unique variety with long, stout stems that can be trained vertically up canes, trellis or other vertical supports – ideal if you've got a small garden and don't want to lose any ground-level space. Stems need tying to supports regularly to prevent them snapping under the weight of dark green fruit.

Bumper crops

It's important to ensure plants are kept well watered to prevent fruit falling off prematurely during dry spells. Boost the production of fruit by feeding plants in pots or in sandy soil weekly with a liquid feed that's high in potash.

To keep plants productive you need to harvest courgettes regularly – expect to be doing this up to three times a week in the height of summer. Remove fruit from stems with a sharp knife, taking care to avoid cutting your hands on the spines that arm some varieties. They are best picked when young – if you leave them on the plant too long they will swell up and taste horrible.

Troubleshooting

Keep a close eye out for slugs and snails, which like to eat the fruit and leaves of young plants, and check for powdery mildew, a fungal disease that leads to a loss of vigour. Remove leaves with a white chalky coating on their upper and undersides, then water and feed plants well to restore their health.

ARE COURGETTES BABY MARROWS?

Due to their similar appearance, courgettes are considered by some people to be baby marrows. This isn't correct. Both are members of the same family, but courgettes have been bred specifically for picking at an earlier stage of growth, while marrows are best eaten when fully mature.

AROUND THE WORLD

The town of Obetz in Ohio, USA, holds an annual four-day Zucchini Festival in August. For enthusiasts, there's a growing competition and plenty of vegetable-based nibbles on offer, such as courgette ice cream!

A little bit of history

Courgettes are believed to have come into use about 7000 years ago in Central and South America. Seeds were brought to Europe by explorer Christopher Columbus and first cultivated in Italy, where it was called zucchino – which roughly translates as baby squash. The British follow the French lead and call it courgette. The vegetable was taken to the USA in the 1920s by emigrating Italians, where it was given the name zucchini.

BIRD CONTROL

There's no doubt that birds are fun to watch, and can be a benefit to gardeners because they will eat pests, but some are a bit of a nuisance in the vegetable garden. Blackbirds will peck at ripe tomatoes, while pigeons will gobble up pea seedlings and strip the leaves of cabbages and other brassica crops, leaving just the stalks and ribs behind.

Traditionally, gardeners have followed the lead set by farmers and placed scarecrows among their crops to discourage foraging birds. These and other deterrents, including DIY solutions such as running strings of shiny CDs across the veg patch, may work for a while but birds often ignore the devices once they get used to them being there.

It's far better to prevent birds getting to vulnerable crops in the first place. Low-growing vegetables can be covered with anti-bird netting. You can place this directly on top of plants and hold it in place with tent pegs. However, birds might still be able to cause damage to the plants where the mesh is in direct contact. A more expensive, but more effective, solution is to fit the netting to tunnel cloches that can be placed directly above plants.

POTAGER

A potager is an ornamental vegetable garden that originates from seventeenth-century France. The kitchen gardens at this time became less utilitarian and more aesthetically pleasing, with a series of geometric beds delineated by lavender, clipped box or wooden edging. These beds were interplanted with a combination of vegetables, herbs and fruit, along with perennial and annual flowers. Edible crops grown in potagers were chosen as much for their attractive leaves, stems, flowers or fruit as for their taste. Supports for beans, gourds, tomatoes and other climbing plants were equally pleasing on the eye, whether rustic or made as a more ornate metal construction. This style of vegetable garden can be incorporated in any-sized garden – even a raised bed in a tiny plot could be turned into a potager. If you need inspiration, there are many good examples to visit. Perhaps the most famous and most extensive is the potager at Château de Villandry in the Loire Valley that covers over 12,500 square metres.

10 attractive vegetables and herbs for potagers

1 **Swiss chard 'Bright Lights'** – rainbow of coloured stems.
2 **Kale 'Black Magic'** – heavily ribbed, dark green leaves.
3 **Bronze fennel** – feathery leaves and plates of yellow flowers.
4 **Lettuce 'Lollo Rossa'** – frilly, red-tinged leaves.
5 **French bean 'Carminat'** – climbing variety with purple pods.
6 **Pak Choi 'Rubi Shine'** – large, reddish-purple leaves.
7 **Courgette 'Atena' F1** – yellow fruit and handsome foliage.
8 **Borage** – blue flowers with cucumber-flavoured leaves.
9 **Chives** – grassy, onion-flavoured leaves and pink flowers.
10 **Globe artichoke** – stately stems and dramatic foliage.

 **LEEKS**

Leeks take up a fair amount of room for a long period of time, but are still worth growing to provide pickings over winter. It's possible to start them from seed during early to mid-spring, but you can save time and space by buying ready-grown seedlings. Plant them in a well-prepared, sun-lit seedbed outdoors. Make holes with a dibber, 20cm deep and 15cm apart, and drop a seedling into each. Pour water into each and let it soak away – this will draw soil over the plant to cover the roots and produce lovely blanched stems. Avoid firming the soil with your fingers.

Aftercare

Weeds will try to colonise bare soil, so remove any you see, avoiding the grass-like baby leek plants – it helps to mark the row so you don't remove any by mistake. Keep plants well watered and feed with high-nitrogen fertiliser in midsummer.

TOP TIP

A T-shaped wooden dibber with a pointy, carbon-steel tip is ideal for planting leeks.

DID YOU KNOW?

Roman emperor Nero thought eating leeks would help improve his singing voice. His nickname was *Porrophagus*, or leek eater!

Blanching

Although the bottom of the leek will be blanched due to being planted in a deep hole, it's possible to extend this tender white area by drawing soil up around the base. Do this carefully to avoid getting any in the leaves.

Harvesting

Leeks will be ready for harvesting between autumn and early spring. Lift as required with a garden fork, taking care to avoid damaging neighbouring plants.

Troubleshooting

Bolting or going to seed early can be a problem – there's nothing for it but to snap off the head. You can avoid this by making sure the crop is not put under stress in dry conditions. Rust is a fungal disease that results in orange pustules appearing on plants – there's no cure, so you will have to lift the infected leeks, remove damaged growth and use the crop as soon as possible. Remember to include leeks as part of a crop rotation to reduce the chances of them being affected by the disease the following season.

RUST-TOLERANT TYPES TO TRY
- 'Porbella'
- 'Autumn Giant 2 – Porvite'
- 'Blauwgroene Winter – Bandit'

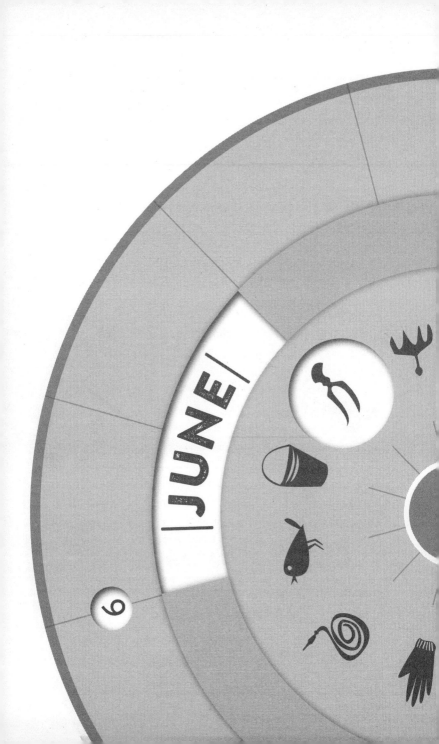

'Although we always hope to see a hot, sunny June, with our variable climate this is not always the case. However, should the weather turn out to be dry then the gardening job which should be at the top of the list now is watering.'

Percy Thrower, *Gardening Month by Month*

Nothing compares to an early summer's day. The weather is warm, but not sticky or oppressively hot, as it can sometimes be later in the season. As the month chugs on and we near the longest day, on 21 June, the days become lighter and seem never-ending. It's fair to say that now all thoughts of winter are completely banished and even the memory of spring is fading fast.

The sun rises very early in the morning and daylight lingers until almost 10 o'clock at night, which encourages plants to grow healthily and provides gardeners with plenty of hours to tend to their needs. Not that all of your time should be spent maintaining your plot, of course, for this is a month in which you should occasionally kick back in the evening and simply enjoy your garden.

There is very little likelihood of frost now, so any tender seedlings still tucked up indoors can now be moved outside. Seeds to be sown now can be put directly into the warm soil, where they'll germinate readily and grow quickly. And if you got a head start on some crops, this is the time when you'll begin to enjoy the fruits of that labour. Early peas, broad beans, salads and, best of all, succulent asparagus spears are ready for harvesting.

Wherever you look, everything is growing with great gusto. Make sure you water both the plants in the ground and in pots regularly and feed them when required so that they remain in rude health. It's important at this stage of the year not to neglect your garden, as things can go downhill quickly if you turn your attention away.

 **CARROTS**

Shops generally stock only a few types, but there's actually a huge variety that can be grown, in many shapes, colours and sizes. Roots can be round, stumpy, conical, slender or candle-shaped and measure between 2.5cm and 30cm. And they're not all orange; white, yellow, red and purple are all available.

When to sow

There are two main groups: early and maincrop. Earlies are ideal for sowing between spring and early summer, and are often ready for harvesting seven weeks later. Sow maincrop varieties from April onwards – these should be ready to lift in 11 weeks, but are tough enough to survive in the ground over winter.

Best early carrots

Early carrots tend to be orange. Among the best are 'Mokum' F1, fast-growing 'Amsterdam Forcing 3' and 'Early Nantes', a French variety with long, cylindrical roots that are tender and sweet.

Best maincrops

There are lots of interesting maincrop carrots to choose from: 'White Satin' boasts tender white roots, 'Jaune de Doubs' is a yellow variety and 'Purple Haze' F1 is a dark purple carrot with an orange core. If you can't decide on a colour, try a seed mix – 'Harlequin' F1 contains white, yellow, purple and orange carrots.

Sowing seeds

Carrots prefer light, stone-free soil in a sunny spot. Prepare the soil by digging, removing weeds and large stones, then rake until the texture resembles fine breadcrumbs. Make a shallow trench, 1cm deep, with the corner of a rake and sow seeds thinly. When germinated, nip off the leaves of weaker seedlings to leave plants 20cm apart. Leave a gap of 30cm between rows.

Looking after them

Keep well watered, especially during periods of dry weather, and remove any weeds. They'll be ready between seven to 11 weeks after sowing, depending on the variety – most will come up easily by hand, but use a fork to prise up those with long roots.

Troubleshooting

Carrot fly is an insect pest whose larvae burrows into the roots of the developing carrots. It's attracted to the scent released by carrots when seedlings are thinned or roots are harvested. It's a good idea to space seeds widely apart to avoid thinning or to nip the foliage off at ground level, rather than yanking out unwanted seedlings. Other options include covering the crop with a sheet of insect-proof mesh or growing a variety with more resistance to carrot fly, such as 'Nandor' F1, 'Sytan' or 'Resistafly' F1.

Growing in pots

Short-rooted varieties are ideal in 20cm pots filled with loam-based compost, such as John Innes No. 2. Scatter seeds thinly over the surface and cover with a 1cm layer of sifted compost. When seedlings have germinated, thin to 4cm apart. 'Chantenay Red Cored 3', 'Mignon' and 'Parmex' all grow in containers.

FOODIE FACT

Carrots are the second most popular vegetable in the world, after potatoes. It's estimated the average Brit eats around 100 a year.

A little bit of history

Native to Afghanistan, the original wild carrots had spindly purple or black roots with a bitter taste. Seeds from these were carried by merchants along trade routes to Europe, Africa and Asia, where larger, tastier and productive roots were developed.

Carrots were considered a potent aphrodisiac by the ancient Romans. Emperor Caligula was particularly taken with them and ordered a range of different dishes made from carrots to be served at a banquet attended by the Roman Senate. He hoped that a civilised meal would turn into a full-scale orgy!

Early cultivated carrots were red, yellow, white and purple in colour and it wasn't until the sixteenth century that the first orange carrots were bred in Holland. During the late nineteenth century, many of the best modern varieties came out of France, such as 'Chantenay'.

Carrots have been grown in Britain since the 1400s, but they only became a staple part of our diet during the Second World War. Unlike many vegetables, they were in plentiful supply and the nation was encouraged to eat them by the Ministry of Food – propaganda posters claimed they'd help you to see in a blackout and a campaign aimed at enthusing kids featured cartoon character Doctor Carrot. Kids were even given carrots on sticks as a substitute for ice lollies!

SWEET POTATOES

Sweet potatoes are an exotic vegetable generally grown from slips, which are long shoots that have been removed from a chitted tuber. You won't often find them for sale in garden centres, but they can be bought from mail-order specialists. They arrive without any roots and are often in need of rehydration. Stand them in a glass of water overnight and then plant them into small pots to establish – ensure the entire length of clear stem is buried. Sweet potato vines are tender, so keep indoors until there's no longer any danger from frost. When roots appear through the bottom of pots they can be planted into vegetable planters or large containers filled with multi-purpose compost.

DID YOU KNOW?

Sweet potatoes are packed with Vitamins A, C and E. They are high in beta-carotene and are a good source of manganese, potassium, copper and other nutrients.

Growing and harvesting

This is a thirsty vegetable, so keep plants well watered and feed every two weeks or so with a general-purpose fertiliser. The plant is related to the climbing ornamental Morning glory and will form long stems that will cascade down the sides of containers. Pinch the tips when they're about 60cm long to encourage bushier growth. In late summer, the foliage will start to yellow and die back. The underground tubers can be lifted immediately, or left until required – ensure that all of them are unearthed before the first frosts.

Sweet potatoes to grow

- 'Beauregard' – medium tubers with salmon-orange flesh.
- 'Georgia Jet' – large tubers with orange flesh.
- 'O' Henry' – cream tubers with golden flesh.
- 'Murasaki' – purple skin and white flesh.
- 'T65' – vigorous. Plum skin and white flesh.

TOP TIP

Ready-grown plug plants are far more expensive than slips, but are easier to grow and, it is claimed, give higher yields.

EDIBLE FLOWERS

Most of us grow vegetables and herbs for their fruit, leaves, stems, roots or tubers, yet many also have edible flowers. Some have a palatable taste and are ideal to add a splash of colour to salads, vegetable dishes and drinks, while larger blooms are perfect for stuffing. Some flowers aren't particularly tasty, but are blessed with the kind of good looks that make them perfect for garnishing dishes.

Chicory flowers are fairly mild and will provide a colourful garnish to salads, while the spicy white flowers of rocket are nice in rice dishes. The trumpet-shaped flowers of courgettes and other plants in the squash family are suitable for stuffing with cheese or other ingredients, before deep-frying.

Dill flowers are great in pickles or fish dishes, chive blooms are perfect added to salads and those from mint can be popped into drinks or savoury dishes. Oregano flowers are quite spicy and good with chicken, bright blue borage flowers are an integral part of a summer fruit cup drink and the tiny white blooms of coriander have a mild coriander flavour.

Not all vegetable flowers are edible, so carry out some research before tucking in – for example, many plants in the Solanaceae family have poisonous flowers, including potatoes, peppers and tomatoes. Others simply taste vile.

CORIANDER

This herb belongs to the Apiaceae family, which also includes parsley, fennel, chervil, celery and carrot. A native of southern Europe, the Middle East and south-western Asia, coriander has been cultivated for over 3000 years. The leaves, seeds and even the roots are used in many ethnic dishes – the latter are often found in Thai food or beaten into curry pastes.

Unlike some herbs, there aren't too many varieties to choose from. However, some have been bred for their leaves while others are better for seed production – these are often ground or added whole to Mexican, Chinese and Moroccan cuisine.

Seeds can be sown directly into well-prepared soil outdoors or into pots filled with multi-purpose compost. Sow thinly and cover lightly. Germination will usually take between 7–20 days. If growing for seeds, thin out to leave a 10cm gap among plants and make sure they are given a sunny site. Plants grown for their leaves are more productive if grown in semi-shade – thin out seedlings to leave 2.5cm gaps.

Cultivating coriander

Growing coriander is really easy. Keep the soil or compost damp, but avoid overwatering – plants in pots are especially vulnerable to bolting, so ensure the compost never dries out completely. It's not really necessary to feed coriander, but the occasional drench with a balanced liquid fertiliser can be used as a pick-me-up if plants are looking sad.

Harvest leaves when they're young, removing the outside stalks first to allow those in the centre to grow. Plants grown for seeds should be allowed to send up long stalks carrying airy sprays of dainty white blooms, followed by peppercorn-sized seeds. Pick when ripe, just before they start to fall to the ground. Cut entire stems and allow to dry on paper. Store them in airtight containers.

What to grow

'Leisure' is a vigorous variety that is slow to bolt and produces masses of leaves; the leaves of 'Lemon' have a citrusy aroma and flavour; *Coriandrum sativum* is good for leaf or seed production.

Make more of supermarket coriander

Pots of supermarket coriander seem to run out of steam quickly, but there's a clever way of making them last longer. Decant the plant and carefully divide the root ball into four smaller portions and replant each into a 5cm pot. Water well and place in a light spot indoors. Don't worry if the stems wilt to begin with – this is perfectly normal and the plant will soon perk up. Avoid picking until it's actively growing. Keep the plants going by moving them into a slightly bigger pot every time roots poke their way out of the drainage holes in the base.

DID YOU KNOW?

In the USA, coriander leaves are known as cilantro. The word coriander is used to describe the seeds.

HOW TO MAKE COMFREY FERTILISER

Off-the-shelf plant feeds can cost a packet, but it's easy to make your own potassium-rich fertiliser to boost flower and fruit production from comfrey leaves, which can be grown from seed or started from ready-grown plants. Ordinary comfrey has a reputation for self-seeding itself around the garden, but *Symphytum* x *uplandicum* 'Bocking 14' is a sterile variety. To make the fertiliser, cut off a few stems, chop them up and stuff them into a large bucket or plastic container – wear gloves if you have sensitive skin as the leaves and stems are covered in hairs, which can irritate some people. Really force the plant material in, adding more until the container is completely full. Fill it up with water. If your container has a lid, pop it on at this point. If not, place the container behind a shed or somewhere else out of the way, as the rotting mixture smells revolting. Allow the leaves and stems to steep for about a month before decanting the brown liquid. Dilute it with 10 parts water before use.

'Gardening is all about enjoying the simple processes, the physical connection with the soil, being creative and moving forward by learning from your mistakes. That's what makes it so special.'

Joe Swift, *Joe's Allotment*

In midsummer, all of the work you put into your garden earlier in the year really comes to fruition. Early potatoes, garlic, onions, carrots, turnips and a host of fresh salads – from crisp radishes to the first outdoor tomatoes – will be ready for harvesting. With good planning, you could be picking something fresh every day and those lucky enough to have a large garden may find they are fairly self-sufficient for the next few weeks. Of course, if you sowed or planted too many of the same kind of vegetables you might be facing a glut. Don't waste the surplus produce – turn them into chutneys, pickles or other preserves, or freeze them for another day or week when they are out of season.

July is generally the warmest month of the year. Many of us like to take advantage of the conditions by striking up the barbecue, enjoying an outdoor meal with friends or simply taking it easy. The days can be long and pleasant, sometimes humid with sticky nights, followed by a thunderstorm the next day. A downpour is welcomed by thirsty plants, but they need so much water to keep them healthy that you should still supplement them by regular watering to ensure their successful growth.

Don't fall into the trap of relaxing too much while enjoying the bounty of your garden. Now is the time to plan ahead for the next few months, so spend some time planting or sowing cauliflowers, Brussels sprouts, Swiss chard, cabbages and many other crops that can be picked in the autumn, winter or even early next spring.

AROMATIC THYME

Thyme is a useful herb, whose edible leaves are used fresh or dried to flavour soups, stews, fish, meat, sausages, stuffing and vegetable dishes. They are also an important ingredient in a classic French bouquet garni and Herbes de Provence.

This large family of plants comes from many different parts of the world, including Britain, but those prized for culinary use tend to originate in the Mediterranean. As you would expect, they like very well-drained soil, lots of sun and a spot that's fairly sheltered from winter wind and downpours. Place a collar of grit around the base of plants in the ground to protect any low-hanging foliage from wet soil.

Another option is to grow thyme in pots. Don't use multi-purpose compost as it retains too much moisture and they hate having damp roots. Plant in free-draining, soil-based compost that has had some horticultural grit mixed in. Allow plants to dry out between waterings and move them into a rain shadow or a sheltered place in winter.

Some good culinary thymes
- **Lemon thyme** (Thymus '*Golden Lemon*')
- **Orange-scented thyme** (T. citriodorus '*Fragrantissimus*')
- **T. pulegioides** ('*Archer's Gold*')
- **Broad-leaved thyme** (T. pulegiodes)
- **T. 'Porlock'**

...and some that are not
Avoid *Thymus pseudolanuginosus, T. serpyllum, T. Coccineus Group* and other creeping varieties. They may be attractive and aromatic, but they are difficult to harvest or have an inferior flavour to other thymes.

 FRENCH BEANS

French beans have spiralled in popularity over recent years, largely due to the wealth of different varieties that are available to grow. Both climbing and dwarf types are available with pods that are flat, round or oval – several are brightly coloured, adding ornamental good looks to the vegetable patch. Many have pods that can be picked young and eaten whole, while others are allowed to mature to allow the seeds inside to be harvested.

Choosing varieties

There are many varieties. 'Cobra' has green cylindrical pods, while 'Pantheon' boasts pretty white flowers followed by flat, juicy green pods. Both are climbers. 'Purple Queen' and 'Purple Teepee' both grow into 35cm tall bushy plants covered with cylindrical purple pods. Similar-sized 'Golden Teepee' and 'Sonesta' have yellow pods, while 'Nomad' is renowned for the outstanding flavour of its green pods.

Growing them

French beans hate cold, damp soil, so are best sown in a sunny, sheltered spot outdoors from mid-spring until the beginning of July. Sow climbing varieties 4cm deep, 20cm apart, in a single row, supporting them in the same way as runner beans. Sow dwarf beans 10cm apart. Both types can be grown in pots – choose a pot that's at least 20cm wide and use a 50/50 mixture of soil-based compost and multi-purpose compost. Construct a wigwam of canes for climbing varieties and sow seeds at the base of each support.

Routine care

Caring for French beans is easy. Water plants frugally until established, increasing the amount you give them after the first flowers appear and until the last of the pods have been picked.

Beans will be ready to pick 8–12 weeks after sowing. Picking regularly, while pods are small and young, will encourage the plant to produce more pods.

WHAT'S IN A NAME?

French bean is an umbrella title for a host of other beans, such as kidney, haricot vert, flageolet, borlotti and string bean.

Borlotti beans

These are a distinctive type of French bean that are a mainstay of Italian cooking. Both climbing and dwarf varieties have highly ornamental green pods that are attractively streaked or splashed with red. Even the beans inside look fantastic thanks to their speckled skin – although sadly this disappears during cooking. The fat, meaty beans can be eaten fresh or are perfect for drying and storing. They can be added to stews and are an integral part of many Italian dishes, such as pasta e fagioli. Commonly known as fire tongue, 'Lingua di Fuoco' has flattish pods heavily streaked red, while 'Lamon' is considered to be the best-flavoured by foodies. 'Supremo' and 'Splendido' are both perfect for pots, forming dwarf bushes little over 60cm tall.

TOP TIP

French beans thrive in fertile soil. If you can, prepare the soil for sowing the previous autumn or winter, digging in plenty of well-rotted manure or garden compost.

STORING HERBS

If you can't keep up with all the leaves produced by herbs, there's no need to let surplus go to waste. Harvest plants and preserve the leaves so they can be used when pickings are likely to be more meagre.

The foliage of rosemary, thyme, sage, bay, lovage, chives, parsley and many other herbs can be dried – if you're not sure if a specific plant can be preserved in this way, check out the dried herb rack at the supermarket to see whether it is offered for sale.

Whole stems of larger plants can be cut and then hung upside down under cover in a dry, airy place. Alternatively, pick individual leaves and lay them on sheets of wire mesh. Leaves need to dry within two days or they will spoil. If the weather is hot and sunny, herbs can be dried in the open air.

To store, once they have dried, break them into smaller pieces and place in airtight containers. It's a good idea to keep all of the used herb jars from the supermarket, which can then be recycled for storing home-grown crops.

Another way to store herbs is to freeze them. Shoots can be cut, placed into freezer bags and labelled. Alternatively, preserve mint, borage, basil, parsley and many others in ice cubes. Wash the leaves, shake them dry, then chop into small pieces and add to an ice-cube mould. Fill with water so that the leaves are completely covered (or they will scorch) and freeze. Whenever you need some herbs for a recipe, simply knock out as many ice cubes as you need and add straight to the pan.

BOLTING

Bolting is a gardeners' term used to describe the action of a plant flowering prematurely, before the crop has been harvested. It's detrimental to the potential yield as the plant diverts all of its energy into producing flowers and then seeds, rather than its edible parts. There are many reasons why this can happen. Environmental changes (such as a drop in temperature), poor soil preparation or sowing too early in the season can all lead to bolting. Also, a lack of moisture during dry periods can put the plant under stress and lead to it running to seed too soon. A wide range of crops can be affected, including lettuce, beetroot, leeks, onions, garlic, rocket, spinach, carrots and members of the brassica family. Plant breeders continue to develop bolt-resistant vegetables, but there are other ways gardeners can avoid problems: prepare the soil well prior to planting; sow or plant outdoors when temperatures pick up in spring; and pay close attention to the growing requirements of individual crops.

HERB CUTTINGS

Thyme, rosemary, marjoram, bay, sage and other perennial herbs are easy to propagate by taking semi-ripe cuttings from now until early autumn.

Cut off a healthy stem, avoiding any with buds on them as they'll put all of their energy into making flowers rather than trying to develop roots. Aim to make 7cm-long cuttings by cutting straight under a pair of leaves with a sharp gardening knife or pair of secateurs. Remove leaves from the lower third of the cutting by pinching them off with your thumb and forefinger. Mix a little horticultural grit into cuttings compost. Fill up a small pot with the compost and make some small holes around the edge with a dibber. Pop a cutting into each, making sure the clear part of the stem is covered. Water and place the pot inside a heated propagator. If you don't have one, cover each pot with a clear freezer bag held in place with an elastic band. The cuttings should have formed roots within a few weeks – when these grow through the drainage holes at the bottom, carefully pot each cutting into its own individual pot.

LUNAR PLANTING

An ancient technique, planting by the phases of the Moon, is enjoying a revival in the twenty-first century. Practitioners believe that the gravitational pull on the Earth at different stages of the lunar cycle has an influence on the way vegetables grow. Essentially the gravitational pull on the ground is strong during the first half of the month, then starts to decrease during the second half.

The lunar month is divided into four different stages or quarters, each lasting about seven days. These are: new moon, second quarter, full moon and last quarter. During the new moon period, the water table rises because the gravitational pull on the Earth is high – this is thought to be the best time to plant leafy crops, such as lettuce, cabbage and cauliflower.

In the second quarter, the gravitational pull reduces but the moonlight is strong. Exponents consider this the key time to plant tomatoes, beans, melons and other fruit-bearing vegetables. The moisture levels in the soil are still OK by the full moon period, although the strength of the moonlight starts to decrease – this is the optimum time for planting root crops.

In the last quarter, water levels recede and the strength of the moonlight is fairly low. Exponents avoid planting anything during this period.

ANCIENT ADVOCATES

First-century Roman naturalist Pliny the Elder wrote in his *Natural History* that the Moon 'replenishes the Earth; when she approaches it, she fills all bodies, when she recedes, she empties them.'

GROW YOUR OWN WASABI

Sometimes called Japanese horseradish, wasabi is an essential part of Japanese cuisine – there's even archaeological evidence to suggest it's been eaten in the country for at least 2000 years. A member of the brassica family, *Wasabia japonica* grows naturally alongside streams in the wild, but is now grown commercially in large glasshouses.

Most people are familiar with the pungent green paste made from grating the swollen rhizome, but all parts of the plant are edible: the petioles, flowers and leaves all carry the same spicy flavour. Sadly, most of the wasabi paste available in the UK is a substandard version made with a tiny percentage of wasabi mixed with horseradish, mustard, starch and bright green food colouring.

The rhizomes are sometimes available in specialist food stores, but the cost is likely to put most people off buying them. If you want to enjoy authentic wasabi without breaking the bank, the answer is to grow it yourself. Young plants can be planted in the soil or grown in pots. They like dappled shade and regular feeding with a general-purpose fertiliser.

It takes two years for the roots to reach maturity. Prior to this, you can pick some of the heart-shaped leaves to add to salads and harvest flowers in the spring – these can be scattered over cold dishes or dipped in tempura batter and deep-fried.

'Fruitfulness and abundance are both optimistic and uplifting. In my own life there's nowhere nicer and few things more wonderful, simply for its oomph, than that prolific growing machine out there, delivering a steady, constant stream of deliciousness into the kitchen.'

Sarah Raven, *The Great Vegetable Plot*

Harvesting vegetables can be a daily event in August, with most of the vegetables started earlier in the year now reaching their peak. It's a pleasure to wander around the garden early in the morning, evening, or whenever you've got the time, with a container to hold all of this home-grown edible treasure. Apart from providing us with plenty of ingredients to transform into wonderful dishes, it's important to keep on top of the picking; many crops will continue to produce more fruit, pods or leaves if they're harvested regularly, while some will simply give up if you don't.

Yet although rewarding, this month is also challenging. This is a time when parents will have their children off school for several weeks and many gardeners take a summer holiday. Neglect the watering, weeding or picking of vegetables for just a few days and you'll return from a well-earned break to find a miserable sight. If you can, enlist a neighbour or friend to continue gathering crops for their own table while you're away. Ask them to carry out watering duties for you, too, or if you have an allotment, rope in a fellow plot holder. If this isn't possible, consider other methods such as an automatic irrigation system.

Days are still warm, but nights become cooler towards the end of the month and activity in the garden noticeably starts to slow down. Plants are now running out of steam and gaps begin to appear more frequently in the vegetable garden after each harvest. There's very little sowing and planting to do this month, but you can fill some of the empty patches with salads and a few other seeds, such as winter purslane and land cress, which will provide food over autumn and winter.

BRIDGING THE HUNGRY GAP

The 'hungry gap' is the term given to a period in spring when there's little or no produce left in store or any that can be picked, unearthed or cut from the garden. This lean time generally occurs in mid-April and can last for six weeks or so before things take a turn for the better. Today, we can buy fresh, frozen or tinned veg from the supermarket to fill the gap but at this time in the past, many people faced great hardship, or even starvation.

The good news is that with a bit of planning in August, you won't have to endure a massive dearth come spring. The key is to grow vegetables that are hardy enough to make it through the winter. A lot can be ruled out, but spinach, chard, leeks, spring cabbage, broad beans and kale are all ideal for sowing or planting now.

For a different taste sensation, try growing some oriental veggies. Despite their exotic origins many are surprisingly hardy and can be grown with little problem if you protect them from the worst of the weather with a cloche or low polythene tunnel. Among the best are Chinese cabbage, tatsoi, pak choi, mizuna, mibuna, Chinese broccoli, choy sum, Oriental mustards and Chinese leaves.

SWISS CHARD

A crop that looks good and tastes good, chard has glossy leaves and brightly coloured stems that are perfect for adding an ornamental touch to the veg patch – in shades of white, red, orange, yellow, pink and purple.

Where to grow it

Swiss chard will do well in sun or partial shade and likes rich, moisture-retentive soil. You can grow it in rows, but its eye-catching appearance means it's great as part of a potager or dotted among other plants in a border. Alternatively, grow it in pots or raised beds.

When to sow it

Seeds sown now will provide leaves for picking over autumn, winter and into spring – for best results, protect the seedlings with cloches, fleece or low tunnels during any cold spells. Seeds that are sown in spring will produce plants that can be harvested in summer.

Sowing seeds

Prepare the soil by making a seedbed. Make a shallow trench, 2.5cm deep, using a garden cane or corner of the rake, then sow seeds thinly along the base. Cover and water. After they have germinated, thin out seedlings so they are about 30cm apart. Space subsequent rows 38cm apart.

Growing in pots

Sow seeds thinly in 7.5cm pots and cover with a 2.5cm layer of compost. When seedlings are 2cm tall, move them into small individual pots. The young plants can then either be planted singly into 12cm-diameter pots or you can put several into a 45cm container.

Looking after plants

Keep plants moist and give them a boost every couple of weeks
with a liquid fertiliser that is high in nitrogen. Weeds will rob
the chard of water and nutrients, so tug out any that appear.

Harvesting

Leaves are ready for picking about 12 weeks after sowing – cut
them off with a sharp knife, starting from the outside of the plant
first. Take care to avoid damage to the roots. Frequent picking
will ensure lots of fresh leaves grow from the centre of the plant.

Five of the best

1 **'Bright Lights'** – a zingy mixture of red, white, orange,
   yellow and pink stems.
2 **'Fordhook Giant'** – large, glossy dark green leaves and
   contrasting white stems.
3 **'Orange Fantasia'** – eye-catching orange stems
4 **'Pink Passion'** – shocking pink stems and dark green leaves
5 **'Ruby Chard'** – glossy green leaves and pillar-box-red stems

A little bit of history

Despite its common name, this leafy vegetable is not a native
of Switzerland. It actually comes from the Mediterranean and
is believed to have developed from coastal sea beet – a plant
that has also given us beetroot. Although it's only become a

fashionable veg here in recent times, it's been in cultivation for thousands of years – a red-stemmed variety was first mentioned by the Greek philosopher Aristotle way back in 350BC. The name chard comes from the French word *carde*, due to the resemblance of the stems to those of cardoon and globe artichoke. Nobody really knows for sure where the Swiss prefix came from, but there are two schools of thought; it could be because the plant was widely cultivated in Switzerland, or that the name was used to differentiate it from varieties of French spinach in nineteenth-century seed catalogues.

> ❛ It grew with me in 1596... which plant nature doth seeme to play and sport herself: for the seeds taken from the plant, which was altogether of one colour and sowne, doth bring forth plants of many and variable colours.' John Gerard, *The Herball* (1636)

TACKLE VINE WEEVIL IN POTS

Vine weevils are the main pests to worry about if you grow perennial vegetables or herbs in pots. The black adult beetles eat notches from around the outside of leaves, but it's their subterranean larvae that cause most damage; they gnaw through roots, checking growth, and in extreme cases the damage can result in a plant collapsing and dying.

The female adult lays hundreds of eggs between April and September, and during this time they can often be found hiding under leaves, beneath pots, in debris or other nooks and crannies. Regularly check these areas and destroy any that you find – it also helps to keep your garden or greenhouse as clean as possible, to reduce the number of hiding places. The beetles are most active after dark and sometimes can be spotted if you go out with a torch.

Rounding up the adults will help, but you're never going to get them all. The best way to prevent their c-shaped, brown-headed larvae from causing harm is to drench containers with a suitable pesticide or, if you prefer an organic approach, to treat with predatory nematodes – sachets containing these microscopic worms can be mixed with water, and applied with a watering can.

How to recognise adult vine weevils

Look out for 1cm-long black beetles with pale brown flecks on the back of their pear-shaped bodies. These slow-moving beetles can't fly, but are capable of walking up vertical surfaces.

And their grubs

Vine weevil maggots are found individually or in groups beneath the compost of damaged plants. They are 1cm long, creamy white with a brown head, and are often curled up in a c-shape.

SALAD ROCKET

Rocket can be raised any time from March, but it's the perfect salad leaf for sowing in late summer when there's very little else that can be grown. Even now, it lives up to its name and will blast into life, rewarding you with piquant leaves within a few weeks.

Growing rocket is easy, whether you want to grow them in the ground or in pots. Outdoors, choose a sunny patch and prepare it with a fork, breaking up large clods and removing any weeds or stones. Next, make a shallow, 1cm-deep groove with the end of a hoe or garden cane and trickle seeds along the base, aiming to space them about 10cm apart. Cover the trench with soil and water.

To raise rocket in pots, almost fill a 30cm container with multi-purpose compost, flatten and lightly scatter seeds across the surface. Don't overcrowd them as they will need thinning to about 10cm apart. Cover lightly with sifted compost and water well, using a can with a rose fitted on the end.

Pick leaves as often as you can from the outside of plants to ensure they produce fresh growth from the centre and water plants regularly to prevent the compost drying out – this can lead to bolting, or running to seed prematurely.

The growing season can be extended outdoors by covering plants with a low polythene tunnel or a cloche when frosty weather looms. Large pots can be moved into a greenhouse, coldframe or front porch. If you want, you could sow seeds in smaller containers to grow on the kitchen windowsill.

Good types of rocket to try

- **'Dragons Tongue'** – bolt-resistant with large leaves marked with purple veins.
- **Wild rocket** – attractive frilly leaves with a pungent taste.
- **'Skyrocket'** – fast-growing leaves with a strong flavour.

A little bit of history

Rocket is a native of Mediterranean regions and was a popular plant among ancient Romans, who would eat the leaves in salads and use the seeds to flavour oil. They didn't just think it was good to eat, though, rocket was considered a potent aphrodisiac – in his poem 'Moretum', Virgil wrote that it 'excites the sexual desire of drowsy people'. Over the last 20 years it's become a trendy salad leaf in the UK, but has actually been grown here since Elizabethan times. It's known by several other names, depending on where you are in the world. The French call it *roquette*, while many Italians know it as *rucola*. In the US, this pungent leafy salad is called arugula.

PLANT PARSLEY

Parsley is an indispensable culinary herb that comes in two main forms – flat and curly leaved. The latter is generally used as a garnish, while the former has a better flavour. This gourmet type is sometimes known as French or Italian parsley.

When to sow

Seeds of this biennial can be sown any time from March to August – early sowings will provide leaves for picking in summer; sowing them in late summer will result in zingy stalks that you can harvest from around February onwards.

Growing in containers

Parsley can be grown in the ground but it's an ideal candidate for growing in containers, especially if you sow later in the year as it's easier to protect the crop then from the worst of the winter weather. Fill a large pot with seed compost and scatter seeds thinly over the surface, aiming to leave about 2.5cm between each – don't worry if some are closer, you can thin them out later. Cover with a 1cm layer of finely sifted compost and water gently using a can fitted with a rose.

Put the pot in a sheltered spot to allow seeds to germinate – a coldframe, greenhouse, front porch or similar place is ideal. Thin out seedlings when they are large enough to handle, leaving about 2.5cm between plants. Water regularly and pick from late winter to ensure a steady supply of leaves.

IF YOU LIKE PARSLEY, TRY THIS...

Par-Cel is a type of celery that has been bred for its leaves. It looks like flat-leaved parsley, but it has a distinct celery flavour.

Look out for leaves that have been
nibbled around the edges to leave a
doily-like effect. This is flea beetle
damage. Prevent problems by
covering developing seedlings with
a sheet of horticultural fleece.

Troubleshooting

Parsley is largely trouble free, but leaves can sometimes turn
yellow if plants are stressed or running short of nutrients. Give
them a pick-me-up by chopping them back to encourage new
growth and feed with a liquid fertiliser. Nip out any flower-
bearing shoots or the leaves will become bitter and inedible.

Top five parsley varieties to grow

1 **'Laura'** – intensely flavoured flat-leaf type.
2 **'Prezzemolo Gigante d'Italia'** – Vigorous flat-leaf
   Italian variety.
3 **'Lisette'** – attractive finely curled leaves.
4 **'Plain Leaved 2'** – one of the best for flavour.
5 **'Aphrodite'** – pretty parsley with tight, curly leaves.

TOP TIP

Parsley seeds are notoriously
slow to germinate. The process
can be accelerated by soaking
the seeds in tepid water the
night before sowing.

'There's absolutely no doubt that you simply can't garden by the calendar. While it's handy to have a list of jobs to be done in the garden just as a memory-jogger, at the end of the day it's the weather and soil conditions that will finally decide when you do things'

Geoff Hamilton, *Gardeners' World Practical Gardening Course*

The first of September marks the arrival of autumn, according to meteorologists, but a change in the seasons isn't always apparent. An Indian summer will see the warm weather often experienced in August extended into October, allowing us to enjoy outdoor living for a while longer. And what a treat it is to be able to continue gardening without the need for bulky knitwear.

Even if the days are warm, night-time temperatures are certainly much cooler than they were last month, leading some to turn on their central heating for the first time. There's also a real possibility, especially if you live further north, that you could wake up to find a frost. Before this happens you need to finish harvesting tender plants grown outside, such as tomatoes, courgettes, peppers and beans. If you're growing tender vegetables in pots and have a greenhouse, you could move them under cover at this time of year to prolong their picking season.

This is a period of great activity in the garden. There are masses of other vegetables to gather, weeds to pull, pests to control and some crops to sow. As plants come to a natural end, the autumn tidy up can begin. Don't waste the debris, though, all of the old foliage, stems, and even roots, can be chopped up and added to the compost heap, where it will turn into a fabulous soil conditioner.

September is also a time to think about wildlife. Many helpful creatures that pollinate our vegetables or devour our pests hibernate in the autumn, so it pays to give them a helping hand through inclement conditions by creating some special habitats for them to hunker down in over the next few months.

GREEN MANURE

Rather than leave a vegetable bed or allotment empty over winter, it's a good idea to sow what's known as a 'green manure' crop. Mustard, winter tares, Hungarian grazing rye, winter field beans and others have many benefits when grown on soil that is going to be free from edible crops for six weeks or more.

These crops will improve the structure of the soil and form a green carpet that stops weeds growing and prevents nutrients being flushed out of the soil by rain or snow. Some types have the ability to capture nitrogen from the air, too, which is released when the plants are eventually dug back into the soil – all of this goodness will give vegetables a boost in spring.

Prepare the empty vegetable bed by removing any weeds and raking the soil level. Scatter seeds over the surface of the soil, following the recommendations on the packet – different varieties need sowing at different rates. Make sure seeds are in firm contact with the soil by tapping the surface gently with the back of your spade, then water well.

Empty patches of soil should be covered by a green carpet within two to three weeks of sowing. Mustard will need digging in later in autumn; the rest can be dug into the soil in spring, or before the plants start to flower. Leave the green manure to decompose in the soil for up to four weeks before growing any vegetables.

WINTER LETTUCE

Tougher weather may be just around the corner, but you can still start to raise lettuces by sowing varieties now that will overwinter. 'Valdor', 'Winter Marvel' and 'Winter Density' are some varieties that are able to cope with cooler temperatures and lower light levels, as long as they are covered with cloches, low polythene tunnels or fleece. Sow directly into the soil, thin out seedlings and provide protection when colder weather arrives. You can either treat the lettuces as a baby leaf crop or allow them to reach full size – expect to be harvesting them between 40 and 70 days after sowing, depending on the weather conditions and the variety you've chosen.

OVERWINTER CHILLI PEPPERS

Chilli peppers are often treated as annuals and discarded at the end of the growing season. However, if you've got a favourite variety it is possible to overwinter them in a frost-free place. Doing this has several benefits; there will be less need to sow chilli peppers in spring (unless you want to try some new varieties) and a ready-grown plant will flower and fruit earlier the following year.

If you're growing them outside, move plants indoors before the first frosts or they'll soon perish. Stand them in a warm, light place, such as a greenhouse, kitchen windowsill or front porch. Strip off any fruit still attached to the branches, then cut the plant back hard to leave a stubby framework about 10cm tall. Remove any leaves to discourage pests and diseases.

Getting the watering regime right is key to their survival. Chilli peppers do not actively grow during winter, so giving them too much water will lead to the roots rotting. Keep them moist by watering every other week, or whenever the compost is on the verge of drying out completely. New leaves should appear in spring and then you can water more regularly. Be warned: this process isn't foolproof and some plants might not make it.

FESTIVE POTATOES

Growing potatoes that can be harvested in winter or, even better, served with your Christmas dinner, is an idea that is becoming increasingly popular in the UK. Many nurseries offer a range of first early or second early tubers that are suitable for planting in pots in early autumn; these include 'Charlotte', 'Maris Peer' and 'Nicola', a lovely spud with a waxy texture and wonderful creamy yellow flesh.

Unlike potatoes started in late winter or early spring, there's no need to chit them first. Simply add a 10cm layer of multi-purpose compost to a 40cm pot or a purpose-built potato-growing container, then place three tubers evenly over the surface. Cover with a 5cm layer of compost and add three more tubers. Cover again and water. Add more compost as the shoots grow, stopping when you have almost filled the container.

The container can go outside at this time of year, but it will need to be moved under cover as soon as there's any danger from frost. Place in an unheated greenhouse, porch, conservatory or a cool front room. Keep the compost damp, but avoid over watering or the tubers will rot.

Earth up the stems as they grow, stopping about 5cm from the top of the pot. Eventually, the haulm, or leafy growth, will produce flowers, turn yellow and die back – usually about 12 weeks after planting. Clear this away and keep the compost dry until you are ready to eat them.

PLANT SPRING CABBAGE

Spring can be a lean time in the vegetable garden, so it's worth planting hardy cabbages now that will be ready for harvesting in April and May. There are lots of different varieties available that will establish themselves over winter, ready to swell quickly during warmer weather and reward you with early, tasty, fat, sweet heads.

Ready-grown spring cabbage seedlings are widely available in the grow-your-own sections of garden centres in early autumn, or for a greater range try an online specialist. Plant them 30cm apart to ensure they have plenty of space to form decent-sized heads. Water well and make sure they never dry out completely or it will check their growth. If stems become exposed due to wind or rain, earth them up to provide stability.

Don't bother feeding plants over winter as nutrients will simply be washed away. Wait until early spring, then give cabbages a boost by drenching the soil around them with liquid feed or by scattering a granular fertiliser around plants. Cabbages should be ready for harvesting from the middle of spring – either pull up entire plants, roots and all, or cut the heads off at ground level.

A potential yield can be ruined if they catch the eye of hungry pigeons. The odd plant can be protected by cloches, but rows are better covered with low tunnels fitted with bird-protection netting. Alternatively, you can drape this material directly over the crop.

Great spring cabbages to try

- 'Pixie' – a compact variety ideal for small gardens.
- 'Duncan' – dark green leaves cover a pointed heart.
- 'Spring Hero' F1 – Roundish, crisp hearts.
- 'Durham Early' – tight pointed heads with a great flavour.
- 'April' – pointed heads and slow to bolt.

PLANT HARDY ONIONS

Japanese or overwintering onion sets can be planted any time between late September and early November. Unlike traditional onions, they are resistant to cold weather and damp soil, and will happily grow during the colder months of the year to produce onions that are ready for harvesting in June and July – around six weeks earlier than those planted in spring. The only downside is the onions don't store well and should be eaten within about four weeks of harvesting. However, they are ideal for filling the gap before maincrop onions are ready. 'Senshyu', 'Radar' and 'Troy' are among the varieties that are available, and they should be planted in exactly the same way as traditional onion sets.

TURN GREEN TOMATOES INTO SOMETHING GOOD

Falling temperatures means any tomatoes left on plants will take longer to ripen and an unexpected frost can wipe out any that remain. Rather than let this happen, pick off entire bunches of green tomatoes and bring them indoors. You could help them turn red by storing them in a paper bag with an apple or banana (it will release a gas that helps them ripen), but a great way of using them up is to turn them into preserves. There are scores of different recipes for chutneys, pickles and relishes. Among the tastiest is sweet green tomato pickle.

You will need

240ml cider vinegar

1kg sugar

1 teaspoon ground cloves

1 teaspoon ground cinnamon

20 green tomatoes, cut into 1cm thick slices

Sterilised storage jars

Combine the vinegar, sugar, cloves and cinnamon in a large pot and bring to the boil. Cook for 1 minute, stirring to dissolve the sugar. Next, add the tomato slices and continue cooking over medium-high heat until they are slightly softened, but still firm (this will take about 5 minutes). Remove from the heat and transfer to sterilised jars. After they have cooled, store in the fridge. They will keep, unopened, for up to six months.

WILDLIFE HABITATS

There can't be many, if any, gardeners who aren't troubled by pests. Whether they suck sap, chomp on leaves, burrow into fruit or spread plant viruses, there's no doubt that there's a legion of critters that are a menace in the vegetable garden.

Nobody wants to resort to chemical sprays, so it pays to make your space more appealing to the kind of beneficial creatures that feed on these less desirable beasts. This is something you can do all year round, but installing habitats in the autumn makes a lot of sense as many creatures will be looking for a snug place to hibernate or roost when the weather turns cold.

A water feature is essential. Birds, small mammals and insects need water to drink, while a pond will become a habitat for a wide range of aquatic insects and amphibians, but keep an eye on these over winter and break any ice that forms.

Some wildlife will find a nook or cranny to hibernate in over winter, but it is a good idea to create some habitats of your own too. Toads, beetles and hedgehogs love to shelter underneath or in gaps of rotting logs. Create a log pile by loosely arranging a few old branches under a tree, at the foot of a hedge or behind a shed.

Alternatively, install a bug box on a wall or fence – these are used by ladybirds, spiders, lacewings and other creatures as a place to shelter or hibernate. There are many available to buy, or you can make your own wooden frame and stuff it with bits of straw, bark, bamboo cane and leaves. Mount on a vertical surface, making sure the box is angled slightly downwards to prevent rain from entering.

DID YOU KNOW?

A pair of adult blue tits can collect up to 10,000 leaf-munching caterpillars for their young.

'The garden at the beginning of October flatters to deceive. The sun still has the heat to warm through your shirt, still carries the tang of summer during the middle of the day. But no one is fooled. This is not the real thing but borrowed from summer, little more than a good memory. Autumn has arrived'

Monty & Sarah Don, *Fork to Fork*

There is a dramatic change in the garden during October. A combination of frosts overnight followed by warm days, lit by a sun glowing low in the sky, will trigger the start of a spectacular display of autumn colour. Pottering in the vegetable patch against a fiery backdrop of yellows, reds, purples and orange is wonderful, but it is a sign that our plots are close to putting up their feet for the rest of the year.

Imminently the branches of trees and shrubs will give up their leaves. They'll flutter down sparsely to begin with, then in greater number as the month progresses or if a gale blows in. Very soon the boughs of some trees will appear bare, although some are more reluctant to give up their treasure and leaves can continue to fall well into winter.

After raking it up, all of this spent foliage can be crammed into bags or stored in wire bins, where it will rot down to form crumbly leafmould. This valuable material can be used as a mulch or dug into the soil to improve its structure.

At the end of October, the clocks go back, depriving gardeners of an hour of evening daylight. For most, this means that any gardening has to be left for the weekend. A key task is to start winter digging. The earlier you start it the better, especially if you have clay soil; it gives frost, rain and snow plenty of time to break down heavy clods.

TIDY UP BEDS

Apart from perennials and winter crops, most plants are likely to have been harvested or are near the end of their useful life, and patches of bare earth, yellowing leaves and spent stems are starting to outweigh any remaining greenery for the first time in many months. It's an inevitable decline. The only solution is to clear the site and to leave it ready for winter digging next month. Pull up annual vegetables that have gone past their best, chop up the stems and add to the compost heap. Do the same to annual plants in pots, then stow away the empty containers. Dismantle wigwams of bamboo canes, A-frame supports used for runner beans and similar structures. Bind the canes with twine and pop them in the shed, ready for next spring.

GARLIC

There are two main types: softneck and hardneck. It's not difficult to tell them apart. Softneck garlic forms a mass of flexible, strappy leaves in the ground, which rise above bulbs with a white, papery skin that encloses lots of small cloves. They are easy to grow and can be stored for months after harvesting. Hardneck varieties form a stiff stalk that is topped with a flower head. Bulbs often don't have an outer skin and the cloves are fewer, but larger in size – the flavour of these is generally preferred by food lovers. Their only drawback is they don't store as well and are best used within a month or so of harvesting.

Among the best softneck varieties is 'Provence Wight', which has large bulbs full of sweet, fat cloves that can be stored until January. 'Arno' has ivory white bulbs and pink cloves with a medium flavour, while 'Solent Wight' is a heavy cropper with large, mild cloves. 'Albigensian Wight' boasts large white bulbs that will keep until February. Of the hardnecks, try mild 'Sicilian Red', strongly flavoured 'Purple Wight' and 'Chesnok Red', its purple-striped bulbs are excellent for roasting whole.

Planting in the ground

Choose a sunny spot. Carefully remove the outer skin of the bulb and separate the cloves – keep the largest, rejecting any that are soft, small, mouldy or show signs of damage. Make small holes in the soil, 20cm apart, and bury each clove so the tip is just beneath the surface – firm them down with your fingertips to prevent birds pulling them up.

Growing in pots

Those who are strapped for space can plant garlic in pots. Fill a 30cm container with multi-purpose compost, then make shallow holes, 10cm apart, around the outside. Place a clove in each, making sure the flat bottom is facing downwards, cover with compost and water.

Taking care of them

As they grow, keep the soil or compost well watered and remove any weeds. Garlic will be ready to harvest in summer when the leaves start to turn yellow. Lift bulbs carefully from the ground with a fork and let them dry naturally in the sun – raise them a few centimetres off the ground to allow air to circulate around them; an easy way of doing this is to place them on a wire rack.

TOP TIP

Don't be tempted to plant garlic from a supermarket. These bulbs are often shipped in from overseas and are unsuitable for surviving winter in our climate. They are also susceptible to disease and some are treated with chemicals to prevent them sprouting.

Storing them

Dried bulbs will keep for a long time if stored correctly. The best way is to arrange a single layer of bulbs in a slatted wooden tray, keeping them in a cool, dry, dark place, such as a shed or garage.

A little bit of history

Native to central Asia, garlic is closely related to leeks, onions, shallots, chives and several other pungent vegetables. It's been cultivated for thousands of years and was popular with the ancient Greeks and Chinese. Archaeologists have even found clay models of garlic bulbs in an Egyptian tomb dating to 3200BC. Garlic (*Allium sativum*) was brought to Britain by the Romans. The indigenous people of Britain called this new foodstuff garleac, an old English word meaning spear plant because of its bolt-upright, pointy foliage. It became a culinary staple but fell out of favour during the sixteenth and seventeenth centuries as the Puritan movement gathered steam – followers were suspicious of the vegetable's strong flavours. It was largely ignored until after the second World War, when an influx of migrants woke up our taste buds with dishes reliant on garlic.

Garlic spray

Garlic isn't just good to eat, it can be used to make a spray to control aphids, whitefly and other pests. Mince 100g of garlic and add to 0.5 litres of water, along with 10ml of washing-up liquid. Mix together well. Strain through a muslin cloth, then dilute the concentrate in 5 litres of water. This mixture doesn't keep well, so use immediately. Remember that garlic is strongly flavoured and residues will remain on plants for up to a month after use. For this reason, it's best to avoid spraying edible plants with this close to harvesting.

MAKE LEAFMOULD

The leaves from deciduous trees will start to fall this month, and will require regular raking to keep your garden tidy. Resist the temptation to put them in the dustbin as the spent foliage can be turned into a rich, crumbly compost which is commonly known as leafmould.

Bags of leafmould aren't cheap to buy, so it makes good sense to create your own supply. When it's partially rotted down, the material can be spread as a mulch around vegetables. If left longer to rot down it will turn into a rich material that contains high levels of humus – this can be dug into the soil to improve its condition and enable it to hold on to moisture.

Which leaves to use

Any leaves can be collected, but hornbeam, oak, beech, sycamore, horse chestnut and the leaves from other deciduous trees rot down really quickly. Those from evergreen trees are best fed through a shredder first, as they can take up to three years to rot down if put in whole. Pine needles are acidic, so are best collected separately to create a mulch for ericaceous plants.

Storing leaves

The best way to store leaves is to make a simple square cage with four tree stakes and a roll of chicken wire – 1m x 1m is ideal. All you need to do is secure the wire to the fence with galvanised U staples. Turn the leaves regularly and ensure the contents of the bin remain moist.

Storing leaves in a small garden

If you have a really small garden, try saving leaves in black plastic bin liners that have been punctured a few times to help drainage and to allow air flow through the bag, preventing leaves turning slimy. Rake up leaves regularly and stash them in the bag. When almost full, ensure the leaves are damp by sprinkling with water, give the bag a good shake and then tie it up. Place in a shady spot out of the way.

When is it ready to use?

When you open the bags next autumn, you'll find the leaves have changed into a crumbly material that is an ideal mulch. Leave it another year and it will rot down further to make a dark brown compost, which can be dug into the ground as a soil conditioner.

GREENHOUSE CARE

If you're planning to use your greenhouse to overwinter herbs or perennial vegetables, or to start off seeds, now is the time to give it some attention. Plants struggle for light during the shorter, duller days, so scrub off shade paint from the exterior with soapy water to ensure as much light as possible reaches the plants inside. Then, remove all of the contents of the greenhouse and give the floor, staging, shelves and every other nook and cranny a good sweep to evict any pests that might be lurking. To make it as snug as possible, fit sheets of UV-stabilised bubble wrap to the interior framework. Check heaters are working. If you've got a paraffin heater, stock up on fuel.

HARDY SALADS

Leafy salads sown during the warmer months of the year can't cope with the cold, but there are a few that can be sown now and are hardy enough to deal with the colder weather that's just around the corner. Seeds can be sown into the ground or into pots, windowboxes or just about any other type of container. Either scatter seeds thinly across the surface of pots, covering with 1cm of fine compost, or sow in short rows if you're using a larger container or sowing into the ground. Water well and wait for them to germinate. Thin out seedlings to around 15cm apart when they are large enough to handle.

Although winter salads are tougher than their summer counterparts, they'll still need a bit of cosseting during a very cold snap. Move under cover and protect plants in the ground with cloches or low polythene tunnels. If your plants are in pots, keep the compost moist, but avoid overwatering to prevent rotting – if you can, put the container in a sheltered spot to prevent it becoming saturated during heavy downpours.

Don't worry if your salads seem sluggish to get going. They won't grow as fast as those sown in summer, so expect to be picking leaves in six to eight weeks' time. To ensure a non-stop supply, sow a fresh batch of seeds every four weeks or so.

DID YOU KNOW?

Winter purslane (*Claytonia perfoliata*) is also known as miner's lettuce. With leaves high in vitamin C, it was eaten by miners during the Californian gold rush (1848–1858) to avoid scurvy.

Good winter salads to grow

- **Winter purslane** – juicy, mild leaves.
- **Texsel greens** – shiny leaves with a taste like spinach.
- **Salad burnet** – deeply divided leaves with a flavour similar to cucumber.
- **Corn salad** – mild-flavoured leaves. Known as lamb's lettuce.
- **Land cress** – peppery leaves which are ideal in shade.

TOP TIP

Don't throw away growing bags after picking summer crops. Cut a panel to expose the compost, then revitalise with slow-release fertiliser granules. Use to sow winter salads.

'We must remember that we get from the garden only what we put into it, and that means effort, time and patience. The soil must be our first consideration. It is not just dirt but something which contains living organisms essential to keep the soil healthy and provide plants with necessary food'

Percy Thrower, *Picture Book of Gardening*

Few months mark their arrival in such an explosive manner as November. Fireworks fill the skies of our towns and cities, while bonfires crackle away on Guy Fawkes Night, warming the exposed faces of any onlookers mesmerised by the flickering flames. Yet there's no such spectacle in the garden. Many trees have been deprived of their autumn splendour, and apart from the odd late-flowering bulb or perennial in our beds and borders, there's very little colour to lift our spirits.

Make the most of dry, sunny days now, there will almost certainly be times when you won't want to step out of the house due to gusty blasts or rain that falls incessantly from leaden skies and chills you to the core. In fact, too much rain will start to wash any nutrients out of soil that you've dug recently, or leave it soggy and difficult to work. If you can, cover the ground with sheets of polythene until there's a break in the weather.

In the vegetable garden there are still plants to harvest. Cauliflowers, kale, cabbages and other brassicas will be a winter staple, but ensure you cover them to prevent hungry pigeons stripping the leaves. Leeks can be pulled from the ground and parsnips lifted after a sharp frost, which helps to improve their flavour. You can also try and beat the weather by growing plants indoors. Flavour-filled micro-vegetables will grow quickly on a light windowsill, while portions of herbs can be dug up, plunged into pots and brought indoors. They'll respond with a flurry of tasty shoots.

WINTER DIGGING

Nothing warms you up on a chilly day than a spot of digging. It's an essential task to ensure the soil is workable and in the best possible condition for the sowing and growing of vegetables in spring.

Why dig?

A freshly turned piece of soil is certainly pleasing on the eye, but there are far more practical reasons why gardeners prepare the soil. During the growing season, soil may become compacted due to foot traffic. This can form a hard layer that impedes drainage, prevents roots penetrating and reduces earthworm activity, among other things. Digging helps to break any hard layers, keeps the soil healthy and also exposes soil-borne pests to hungry birds. Frost will lend a helping hand in breaking down heavy clods of earth – although you can dig the soil any time over winter, or even in early spring, if you don't have time now. The earlier you do it, the more chance frost has to work its magic.

The three main types of digging

1   **Simple digging** – Good for cultivating areas around permanent plants.

    Technique: Remove a clod, turn it over and drop it back into the ground. Chop it up a bit with your spade. If you have very stony or heavy clay soil, it's often easier to do this with a garden fork.

2   **Single digging** – Good for soil that's regularly cultivated.

    Technique: Start at one end of the area to be dug and excavate a trench to the depth of the spade's blade – a measurement known as a spit – about 25cm long. Use a wheelbarrow to move the soil to the other end of the area.

Add manure or garden compost to the bottom of the trench, then dig out another and drop the soil removed into the first one. Carry on like this until you reach the end, removing perennial weeds and burying annuals as you go. The final trench can be filled with the soil you moved earlier.

3 **Double digging** – Good for uncultivated or poorly drained land.

Techique: Similar to single digging, except soil is cultivated to the depth of two spits. There are several ways of doing this, but the least labour-intensive one is to cultivate the second spit in-situ. To do this, excavate soil from the first trench and set aside. Loosen the base with a fork, pushing the tines (prongs) into the ground as deeply as possible. Dig out another trench and drop the soil into the gap left by the first. Loosen the base of the second trench as before and carry on like this until you reach the end. Use the soil from the first trench to fill the final trench.

Safe digging

To avoid accidents it's best never to dig when the soil is frozen or waterlogged and to wear boots with reinforced toecaps. Stretch for a few minutes to warm up the muscles and avoid straining anything before you begin. As you dig, keep your back straight, bend at the knees and avoid lifting too much with the spade at once. If you have a large area to dig, don't try and do it all at once. Spread the work out over several weeks, and take regular rests. Remember, it's not a race.

'No-dig gardening'

This quite simple method means that the soil is left unturned. Instead, a layer of compost is spread over the vegetable bed each year, where it provides food for worms and helps to maintain structure and soil fertility. In order to prevent the soil structure being damaged, exponents avoid walking on the beds and manage their plants from paths along the side. The technique is widely associated with organic gardening and has been promoted as an alternative to traditional digging since the middle of the twentieth century following the publication of two key books: *Is Digging Necessary?* by F.C. King (1946) and Albert Guest's *Gardening Without Digging*, published in 1948.

DID YOU KNOW?

Double digging used to known by the far more colourful name of bastard trenching!

A LITTLE BIT ABOUT SPADES...

The word spade is derived from the Anglo-Saxon spadu. It's been an essential digging tool for a long time and although its shape has changed very little, the materials used have. In the Bronze Age, wooden-bladed spades were used for mining, while Romans used heavy cast-iron versions. In medieval Britain, spades were made from a single piece of wood with the blade edged with iron to give it strength. During the Victorian period, spades with a D-handle grip were popular in the south of Britain, while T-handled tools were more often used in the north of the country.

OUT-OF-SEASON HERBS

Many useful herbs that are growing outdoors will die back when the weather turns chilly, but you can trick some of them into producing fresh leaves by moving them indoors. Mint is the one of easiest to force into growth. Dig up a few healthy roots and cut them into 10cm-long pieces with a sharp knife. Fill a 15cm pot with multi-purpose compost and lay a few pieces of root lengthways along its surface. Lightly cover with compost, water and place on a light, warm windowsill or inside a heated greenhouse. Keep the compost barely moist until the shoots appear – within a couple of weeks. Oregano, tarragon and several others will respond in a similar way. If they're growing in the ground, lift clumps, pot them up and place in a well-lit spot under cover. This is even easier to do with plants already growing in pots. Simply clear away any decaying foliage and stems, then place the pot in a warm, bright spot until new leaves appear.

Prepare herbs and vegetables in pots for winter

When the weather is foul outside we can duck indoors, but perennial vegetables or herbs in pots don't have it so easy. Plummeting temperatures, frost and rain can cause roots to die or rot. And it's not just the plants that are vulnerable – a hard frost can lead to expensive terracotta or ceramic pots cracking and falling apart.

Move plants to a more sheltered spot, ideally within the rain shadow of a wall or fence, to prevent the compost getting too wet. Reduce problems further by raising containers up on 'pot feet'. These may be made from terracotta, stone or cast-iron. Some are wedge-shaped, while others are more elaborate, but they all do the same job. Put three under a container to raise it about 2.5cm or so above the ground, allowing excess moisture to escape through the drainage holes. The gap under the pot will also give plants a boost, by providing better air circulation to the root area. Frost can easily penetrate the sides of containers and kill roots or cause the surface to crack, so wrap the entire exterior with a piece of hessian or bubble wrap, ensuring it's held securely in place with garden twine – keep the top of the pot free of material so you can continue to water the plant.

GROWING BROAD BEANS

Freshly picked broad beans are a taste sensation. The young beans are sweet, tender and succulent. Although they are generally sown between March and April, it's possible to sow some varieties in late autumn for a crop that is ready to harvest much earlier. Plants that are started now also tend to mature before blackfly appear in late spring or early summer and weaken plants and reduce yields by sucking at their sap.

Sowing in autumn is ideal if you have a sheltered garden in the south of the country, but those with heavy clay soil or who live in a colder area or have an exposed plot should delay sowing until spring or be prepared to protect young plants with cloches during periods of bad weather.

Not every variety of broad bean is suitable for sowing in autumn, so check the packets and pick carefully to ensure they can cope with conditions over winter.

Sowing seeds

Fork over the soil, removing any weeds and large stones. Rake to leave a fine finish. Sow seeds in rows in shallow trenches 5cm deep, spacing seeds 23cm apart. Leave a gap of 60cm between rows. Cover and water well. Sow a few extra seeds at the end of each row to act as a safeguard against any not germinating. These can be lifted and replanted into a better position if necessary.

Looking after plants

Keep plants well watered, especially when pods appear and during periods of dry weather. Pinch out the growing tips of each plant as pods begin to develop to encourage them to produce more beans. If you sow a variety that grows over 45cm high, you'll need to support stems with garden canes, tying them in with lengths of string.

Harvesting

You can pick pods when they are 7.5cm long and cook them whole. When picking pods to shell, wait until the beans are visible through the pod, but don't leave them too long – the scar on the bean should still be white or green, not black, as the beans will be tough at this stage.

Troubleshooting

Look out for black bean aphid. Sowing early should avoid problems, but it's no guarantee. Whatever time of year you sow, pinch out the top 7.5cm of the stems when the first pods start to form, as aphids are attracted to this fleshy growth. If you do have problems, use a pesticide containing pyrethrum, plant or fish oils, or thiacloprid.

Growing in pots

Early to mid-spring is the best time to sow broad bean seeds in pots. Choose a compact variety and a container that's at least 45cm wide by 25cm deep. Fill with multi-purpose compost and sow seeds 5cm deep, 10cm apart.

A few good varieties

Autumn sowing

- 'The Sutton' – a compact, hardy variety that doesn't require support.
- 'Aquadulce Claudia' – long pods full of tender, sweet beans (can also be sown in early spring).
- 'Witkiem Manita' – fast-growing with long pods (can also be sown in spring).

Spring sowing

- 'Crimson Flowered' – a bean that not only tastes good but looks good too, thanks to its purply-red flowers.
- 'Stereo' – tender-skinned beans that can be cooked like mangetout.

A little bit of history

Broad beans (*Vicia faba*) are believed to have originated from the Middle East and are thought to have been cultivated since 6000–6500BC. In ancient Egypt the Pharoahs considered them to be an inferior foodstuff suitable only for feeding to slaves, while the ancient Greeks considered them good to enough to offer to their god Apollo. The Romans also held them in high regard, and in the Senate broad beans were used to cast votes: a white bean meant yes, a black bean meant no. In Britain, the broad bean was the most widely cultivated bean until runner beans and other species arrived from the New World during the fifteenth century.

CULTURE VULTURE

Broad beans are also known as fava beans in some countries. Film buffs will always associate them with Hannibal Lecter, the cannibal anti-hero of *The Silence of the Lambs*, who says: 'A census taker once tried to test me. I ate his liver with some fava beans and a nice Chianti'.

CHECK ON STORED CROPS

Some crops will keep for ages if stored correctly, but to paraphrase the saying, all it takes is one bad apple (or vegetable, in this case) to spoil an entire sack or boxful. It's astonishing how quickly a single mouldy veggie can contaminate its close neighbours, so it's best to get into the habit of regularly checking potatoes, onions, carrots, cabbages and anything else you've managed to squirrel away, removing any crops that show obvious signs of rot or damage, or that feel softer than the rest when squeezed. Try not to be heavy-handed when you inspect your produce: avoid bruising or damaging the vegetables, which is likely to encourage their deterioration when placed back in storage. Apart from impromptu health checks, do a quick scan of your stored vegetables every time you remove any for use in the kitchen.

'Keeping plants going from year to year, whether through cuttings or protection from the elements, is all part of the skill and fun of being a gardener.'

Tony Buckland, *Flowers*

There will probably have been times in the past year that you've bemoaned the lack of hours in the day available to tend to your vegetables, and then in December you'll find you have plenty of time on your hands but nothing to do. It's simply the quietest month of year with nothing really to sow, plant or maintain. This is probably just as well, though, as this month most of us find ourselves buying gifts, preparing food and getting our homes ready for the festive season.

If you planned well earlier in the year there will still be some crops outdoors that can be harvested. Adding some of your own veggies to a seasonal feast makes it much more personal and everyone around the table will appreciate it all the more, so don't be shy in letting them know their origin! Hardy salads grown under cloches or cold frames are most welcome in winter, while brassicas and many root crops will be at their best after a good frost, which will improve their flavour. Beyond these, though, you can fall back on crops you have stored away for the winter.

The weather is often cold, wet, windy and sometimes even snowy during December. If you do get a fine sunny day and you are itching to do something useful, you could spend it tidying up the shed or greenhouse, or cleaning tools. It will save you loads of time in spring when you will want to get on with more important tasks.

Apart from Christmas Day, there's another date to celebrate near the end of the month – the shortest day of the year, which falls on 21 December. After this the days will start to lengthen again, so you can start dreaming now of what you're going to do in the New Year.

SUPER-FAST MICROGREENS

If you have space on a windowsill, greenhouse or another light spot indoors, try growing microgreens. Also known as micro leaves, living greens and micro herbs, they are the easiest and fastest crops you can grow.

Essentially a vegetable or herb seedling that's picked soon after germination, they pack a more intense flavour than they would if they were fully grown. Seedlings are perfect for perking up salad dishes or for use as a tasty and eye-catching garnish – in fact, they are highly prized by chefs and are expensive to buy from specialist food shops.

They can be raised indoors all year round, but are a perfect winter crop as most gardeners will be busy with outdoor edibles in a few months' time. Seedlings sown during the cooler months, when daylight hours are shorter and light intensity is lower, will take longer to develop then those sown during the spring and summer.

Sowing seeds

Shallow seed trays are the perfect shape and size for microgreens, as these crops don't need a deep root run, and it also enables you to produce a large number of seedlings. Alternatively, recycle old plastic containers or punnets, making sure to puncture some drainage holes in the base.

Add a 5cm layer of seed compost to the bottom of the container and gently flatten it. Scatter your chosen seeds fairly thickly over the surface so they are almost touching. Cover with a thin layer of finely sifted compost. Pour some water into a bigger tray that you can place the seed tray in and allow it to soak up the liquid until the top of the compost is damp.

Looking after plants and harvesting

Place the tray on a drip tray on a light, bright windowsill in a warm room. Add more water whenever the compost dries out and harvest the seedlings when they've formed their first seed leaves (cotyledons). Either snip them off at ground level with a pair of scissors or pull the whole thing out, roots and all, and wash thoroughly before serving.

What to grow

Coriander, chervil, chives, spring onions, broccoli, rocket, celery, peas and many other herbs and vegetables are worth trying for the intense flavour of their leaves. Basil tastes great, but it is better sowed in summer. Apart from tasting good, purple radish, red mustard, beetroot and Swiss chard 'Bright Lights' look fantastic on the plate due to their coloured stems.

TOP TIP

Pea seeds are protected by a water-resistant seed coat that makes them tricky to germinate. Soak them in water overnight to improve germination.

LIMING SOIL

If you have an allotment you might hear some of the older gardeners talking about 'sweetening the soil' with lime. This is something vegetable gardeners have done for generations to increase the alkalinity of acidic soils. Why? Cabbages and other members of the brassica family are vulnerable to club root, a fungal disease that is more prevalent in acidic soil, causing stunted growth and wilting.

Determine whether you need to lime your soil by checking its pH with a testing kit. There's a range of devices available, which vary in their sophistication, but most work the same way. A soil sample is added to a test tube, followed by a chemical powder, then you simply add a little water and give the whole thing a shake. The solution changes colour and you can check the pH against a colour-coded chart. A pH of 7.0 is neutral, anything above this is alkaline and anything below it indicates that you have acid soil.

If you have acidic soil it's probably best to spread some garden lime (calcium carbonate) over the area. Wear gloves and goggles when you do this, and rake it gently into the soil surface. The amount you apply depends on your soil type, so follow the instructions on the back of the packet. Aim to lime your soil two to three months before planting so it has a chance to break down in the soil and won't damage young growth.

PLANTS IN THE BRASSICA FAMILY

Broccoli	Kohl rabi
Brussels sprouts	Mustard
Cabbage	Radish
Cauliflower	Swede
Kale	Turnip

BIRD-FRIENDLY GARDEN

Birds are described as a gardener's best friend for good reason. They are important allies in the battle against all of those pests that like to munch on the crops in our gardens. Many different types of birds vacuum up aphids, thrushes are partial to snails and an adult blue tit is capable of collecting up to 10,000 caterpillars or grubs for its young.

To attract birds into the garden it's important to get the planting right. Try to cover your vertical surfaces with climbers or wall shrubs, whose branches and foliage will offer shelter, cover and nesting spots and the insects that take refuge beneath it make tasty pickings for hungry beaks.

Taller shrubs provide places in which birds can lie low if they become alarmed and are necessary if you want more cautious species to come into your garden. Penstemons, buddleia, hebes, lavender and other nectar-rich flowers will attract insects which in turn will entice hungry birds.

Install a number of different feeding stations, such as a traditional bird table, a lower-level feeding table, and hanging feeders placed in trees or on special supports. There are lots of different seed mixes available; some are aimed at attracting specific types of birds and others are general mixes, packed with high-energy food and essential oils. Remember to top up birdbaths regularly and remove any ice.

COMPOSTING

Over the course of a year our homes and gardens generate a lot of what's known as green waste. Councils often collect this material, but it's far better to recycle it yourself by turning it into garden compost. When tree and shrub prunings, spent multi-purpose compost from containers, dead-headed flowers, fallen leaves, lawn clippings, vegetable peelings and similar materials have rotted down, they form a dark brown, moist, crumbly substance that actually smells quite sweet. It can be used as a mulch, soil improver or, if you're particularly adventurous, you could even use it as a constituent for your own compost mix for pots.

A good time to start

In principle you can start composting at any time of the year, but autumn and winter is a good time to install a bin as you can use it to collect waste during the next few months. Also, most gardeners can find some time to spare during the cooler months – in a few weeks' time you may find you've got far too much on your plate to think about composting.

A choice of bins

There are several different types of compost bin. Plastic and wooden bins are available from garden centres in many shapes and sizes. Some of these are fairly ornamental, such as those resembling beehives, and expensive, but you don't need anything fancy to compost waste – a home-made bin will suffice. These can be made from pallets, breeze blocks or by constructing a simple square cage – attaching wire netting to four stout posts hammered into the ground. Ideally, place two or three bins alongside each other. This will allow you to continue filling one, while using the contents of another. If you haven't got the space, don't worry, one bin is better than none at all.

Place compost bins in a shaded,
sheltered spot, so they don't dry out
too quickly. Ornamental bins can
be left in view, but others are best
hidden – avoid putting them in a part
of the garden that's hardly visited
otherwise it won't get much use.

How to make a pallet compost bin

It's quick and easy to make your own compost bin. All you need is four flat wooden pallets, six stout tree stakes, a mallet and some wire. Place the bin on weed-free, fairly level ground.

1   Stand a pallet on its side to form the back of the bin. Fix it to the ground by easing two stakes into the gap between its layers. Make sure you have one at each end and hammer them firmly into the ground.

2   Stand a pallet at a right angle to the one already in place and fix with stakes as before. Make sure it's nestled in tightly to prevent compost falling through a gap in the corner. Do the same on the other side with the remaining pallet to form a three-sided structure.

3   Strengthen the bin by binding the corners together with some wire.

4   Make a door for the structure with the remaining pallet. Secure it to one side with wire so it can be opened and closed as required.

How composting works

To rot the materials effectively, the compost heap needs a combination of air, moisture and nitrogen, which will encourage bacteria to break down the organic material. As it starts to decompose, temperatures between 50–70°C can be reached in the centre of the heap – 60°C is enough to kill any weed seeds, while 50°C will kill a number of pests and disease pathogens that might be present in the mix. Composting will slow down or even stop in dry or cold weather. Sprinkle the mix with water in periods of drought and cover with a piece of plastic sheeting, cardboard or an offcut of carpet to keep it warm in winter and to prevent excessive rain making it too wet.

A good mix

Generally waste is split into two groups: greens and browns. Sappy plant material that rots down quickly falls into the green camp – it provides nitrogen and moisture to the mix. Browns are drier materials that are rich in carbon and provide fibre and give the compost structure. On their own, greens produce a smelly sludge, so a good compost mix will contain a greater percentage of brown material. Add materials in layers up to 10cm deep, and turn the heap regularly with a fork.

What to compost

Prunings, shredded twigs and branches, dead-headed flowers, lawn clippings, annual weeds that haven't formed seed heads, coffee grounds, tea bags, vegetable peelings, fruit skin, paper and cardboard, egg shells, exhausted bedding plants, dried leaves.

And what you shouldn't compost

Pet or human faeces; meat, fish, dairy or any cooked kitchen waste; diseased or pest-infested plant material; dock, bindweed and any other perennial weeds; large woody prunings should be fed through a shredderbefore adding to compost.

Wormeries

Don't worry if you want to make compost but don't have space for a traditional heap, wormeries can be tucked into the smallest of gardens as they are extremely compact, with one of the top-selling kits in the UK measuring around 74cm high by 48cm wide. It's a clever system that comprises of a four-tiered tray that sits on a tripod. To set it up, fill the first tray with some damp coir, then add the special composting worms that come with the kit.

Vegetable peelings, tea bags, banana skins, coffee grounds, bits of waste bread, egg shells, the odd flower head and bits of newspaper can then be sprinkled on top of the coir. It's best to shred or cut everything up into small pieces first, which will help the material break down faster. A lid placed on top will keep it dark for the worms inside and a waterproof cover will prevent rain making the mix soggy.

When the tray has been filled and the worms have eaten their way through all the waste to leave behind a dark brown compost, they will migrate to the next tray up, which can be filled as before. Continue to add material until the third tray has been filled.

Apart from the compost, there is a sump at the bottom that collects liquid from the rotting vegetable matter that is known as worm tea, due to its brown colour. This can be siphoned out by a tap and diluted with water to be used as an organic plant food.

WHEN TO SOW & PLANT CHART

VEGETABLES

Asparagus

	J	F	M	A	M	J	J	A	S	O	N	D
Plant crowns			X	X								
Harvest				X	X							

Aubergines

	J	F	M	A	M	J	J	A	S	O	N	D
Sow		X🏠	X🏠	X🏠								
Harvest							X	X	X	X		

Beetroots

	J	F	M	A	M	J	J	A	S	O	N	D
Sow			X🔺	X	X	X	X					
Harvest						X	X	X	X	X		

Broad Beans

	J	F	M	A	M	J	J	A	S	O	N	D
Sow			X	X						X	X	
Harvest						X	X	X				

 = Sow indoors

 = Sow undercover

Cabbages, spring

	J	F	M	A	M	J	J	A	S	O	N	D
Sow							X	X				
Plant out									X	X		
Harvest		X	X	X								

Carrots

	J	F	M	A	M	J	J	A	S	O	N	D
Sow				X	X	X	X	X				
Harvest						X	X	X	X	X	X	X

Cauliflowers, autumn

	J	F	M	A	M	J	J	A	S	O	N	D
Sow				X🏠	X🏠							
Plant out						X	X					
Harvest							X	X	X	X		

Courgettes

	J	F	M	A	M	J	J	A	S	O	N	D
Sow				X🏠	X🏠							
Plant out					X	X						
Harvest							X	X	X	X		

French Beans

	J	F	M	A	M	J	J	A	S	O	N	D
Sow				X	X	X	X					
Harvest							X	X	X	X		

Garlic

	J	F	M	A	M	J	J	A	S	O	N	D
Plant	X	X	X							X	X	X
Harvest					X	X	X	X				

Jerusalem Artichokes

	J	F	M	A	M	J	J	A	S	O	N	D
Plant tubers		X	X	X								
Harvest	X	X	X							X	X	X

Kale

	J	F	M	A	M	J	J	A	S	O	N	D
Sow				X⌂	X⌂							
Plant out					X	X	X					
Harvest	X	X	X	X							X	X

Leeks

	J	F	M	A	M	J	J	A	S	O	N	D
Sow				X🏠	X🏠							
Plant out				X	X	X						
Harvest	X	X	X	X					X	X	X	X

Onions

	J	F	M	A	M	J	J	A	S	O	N	D
Plant sets			X	X								
Harvest								X	X			

Onions, hardy

	J	F	M	A	M	J	J	A	S	O	N	D
Plant sets									X	X	X	
Harvest						X	X					

Peas

	J	F	M	A	M	J	J	A	S	O	N	D
Sow			X🔺	X	X	X	X					
Harvest							X	X	X	X		

Potatoes, first early

	J	F	M	A	M	J	J	A	S	O	N	D
Plant tubers			X	X								
Harvest					X	X	X					

Potatoes, second early

	J	F	M	A	M	J	J	A	S	O	N	D
Plant tubers				X								
Harvest						X	X	X	X			

Potatoes, main crop

	J	F	M	A	M	J	J	A	S	O	N	D
Plant tubers				X								
Harvest									X	X	X	

Pumpkins and Winter Squash

	J	F	M	A	M	J	J	A	S	O	N	D
Sow				X🏠								
Plant out					X	X						
Harvest										X		

Runner Bean

	J	F	M	A	M	J	J	A	S	O	N	D
Sow				X🏠	·X🏠							
Plant out					X	X						
Harvest							X	X	X	X		

Shallots

	J	F	M	A	M	J	J	A	S	O	N	D
Plant sets		X	X									
Harvest							X	X				

Sprouting Broccoli

	J	F	M	A	M	J	J	A	S	O	N	D
Sow		X🏠	X🏠	X🏠								
Plant out					X	X	X					
Harvest	X	X	X						X	X	X	X

Squash, summer

	J	F	M	A	M	J	J	A	S	O	N	D
Sow				X🏠								
Plant out					X	X						
Harvest						X	X	X	X			

·Sow from Mid May

Sweet Potatoes

	J	F	M	A	M	J	J	A	S	O	N	D
Plant slips			X🏠	X🏠	X🏠	X						
Harvest								X	X	X		

Sweetcorn

	J	F	M	A	M	J	J	A	S	O	N	D
Sow					*X	**X						
Harvest							X	X	X			

Swiss Chard

	J	F	M	A	M	J	J	A	S	O	N	D
Sow				X	X	X	X	X				
Harvest		X	X				X	X	X	X	X	

Tomatilloes

	J	F	M	A	M	J	J	A	S	O	N	D
Sow		X🏠	X🏠									
Plant out				X	X							
Harvest								X	X	X		

*Sow from Mid May
**Sow from Early June

SALAD VEGETABLES

Lettuce, winter

	J	F	M	A	M	J	J	A	S	O	N	D
Sow								X	X	X		
Harvest	X	X	X	X	X					X	X	X

Rocket

	J	F	M	A	M	J	J	A	S	O	N	D
Sow			X	X	X	X	X	X				
Harvest				X	X	X	X	X	X	X	X	

Sprouting Seeds

	J	F	M	A	M	J	J	A	S	O	N	D
Sow	X⌂	X⌂	X⌂	X⌂	X⌂	X⌂	X⌂	X⌂	X⌂	X⌂	X⌂	X⌂
Harvest	X	X	X	X	X	X	X	X	X	X	X	X

Salad Leaves, hardy

	J	F	M	A	M	J	J	A	S	O	N	D
Sow								X▲	X▲	X▲		
Harvest	X	X	X								X	X

Salad Leaves, mixed

	J	F	M	A	M	J	J	A	S	O	N	D
Sow			X▲	X	X	X	X	X	X▲			
Harvest					X	X	X	X	X	X		

Microgreens

	J	F	M	A	M	J	J	A	S	O	N	D
Sow	X🏠	X🏠	X🏠	X🏠	X🏠	X🏠	X🏠	X🏠	X🏠	X🏠	X🏠	X🏠
Harvest	X	X	X	X	X	X	X	X	X	X	X	X

Tomatoes

	J	F	M	A	M	J	J	A	S	O	N	D
Sow			X🏠	X🏠								
Plant out					X	X						
Harvest							X	X	X	X		

Cucumbers, indoors

	J	F	M	A	M	J	J	A	S	O	N	D
Sow		X🏠	X🏠	X🏠								
Plant					X							
Harvest							X	X	X	X		

Cucumbers, outdoors

	J	F	M	A	M	J	J	A	S	O	N	D
Sow				X▲								
Plant out					X	X						
Harvest							X	X	X			

Radishes

	J	F	M	A	M	J	J	A	S	O	N	D
Sow			X	X	X	X	X	X	X			
Harvest					X	X	X	X	X	X		

Peppers, Chilli and Sweet

	J	F	M	A	M	J	J	A	S	O	N	D
Sow		X▲	X▲									
Plant out					X	X						
Harvest						X	X	X	X			

HERBS

Basil

	J	F	M	A	M	J	J	A	S	O	N	D
Sow		X🏠	X🏠	X🏠	X🏠	X🏠						
Plant out					X	X	X	X				
Harvest						X	X	X	X	X		

Chives

	J	F	M	A	M	J	J	A	S	O	N	D
Sow			X🏠	X🏠	X🏠							
Plant out					X	X	X					
Harvest					X	X	X	X	X	X		

Coriander

	J	F	M	A	M	J	J	A	S	O	N	D
Sow				X	X	X	X					
Harvest						X	X	X	X			

Parsley, in pots

	J	F	M	A	M	J	J	A	S	O	N	D
Sow			X	X	X	X	X	X				
Harvest	X🏠	X🏠	X	X	X	X	X	X	X	X	X🏠	X🏠

Rosemary

	J	F	M	A	M	J	J	A	S	O	N	D
Plant out				X	X	X	X					
Harvest	X	X	X	X	X	X	X	X	X	X	X	X

Thyme

	J	F	M	A	M	J	J	A	S	O	N	D
Plant out				X	X	X	X					
Harvest	X	X	X	X	X	X	X	X	X	X	X	X

OTHER HELPFUL BOOKS

Flowers by Toby Buckland (BBC Books, 2011)

Fork to Fork by Monty and Sarah Don (Conran Octopus, 2009)

Gardening at Longmeadow by Monty Don (BBC Books, 2012)

Gardening Month-by-Month by Percy Thrower (Littlehampton Book Services Ltd, 1984)

Gardeners' World Practical Gardening Course by Geoff Hamilton (BBC Books, 2000)

Joe's Allotment by Joe Swift (BBC Books, 2009)

Life in a Cottage Garden by Carol Klein (BBC Books, 2011)

Percy Thrower's Picture Book of Gardening by Percy Thrower (Collingridge Books, 1968)

The Complete How to be a Gardener by Alan Titchmarsh (BBC Books, 2005)

The Edible Garden by Alys Fowler (BBC Books, 2010)

The Great Vegetable Plot by Sarah Raven (BBC Books, 2011)

The Kitchen Gardener by Alan Titchmarsh (BBC Books, 2008)